THE FISHING WIDOW'S GUIDE

THE FISHING WIDOW'S GUIDE

Rosie Barham

ROBSON BOOKS

First published in Great Britain in 1995 by Robson Books Ltd,
Bolsover House, 5–6 Clipstone Street, London W1P 8LE

British Library Cataloguing in Publication Data
A catalogue record for this title is available from the British Library

Book design by Harold King
Illustrations by Mike Strudwick

ISBN 1 86105 007 0

Typeset in Meridien by Columns Design and Production Services
Ltd, Reading
Printed in Great Britain by WBC Book Manufacturers Ltd,
Bridgend, Mid-Glamorgan

For my own, special anglers: Derek, Dave and Simon, nephews Paul Brockett and Dan Barham – and fishing widows everywhere.

Thanks to: Cliff Brown, editor of *Improve Your Sea Angling*, for his sense of humour and kindness; Terry Doe, my mentor and literary friend, for his support and encouragement; Tim Paisley, editor of *Carpworld*, for inspiration and advice; Adam Smith, editor of *Airgun World*, for taking a chance on an unknown writer; Nick Fisher, for a metaphorical kick up the backside; Louise Dixon of Robson Books, for her enthusiasm towards my work; and especially my mother, Rose Bartlett, who washed dishes, ironed shirts and made coffee while I scribbled.

Contents

Part One: *Gone Fishin'?*

Part Two: *The Carp Widow*

Part Three: *The Coarse Widow*

Part Four: *The Sea Widow*

Part Five: *Serendipity*

PART ONE

Gone
Fishin'?

Why?

There are times when it's not easy for we fishing widows to maintain an equilibrium while living in an angling household. We complain, don't we? Sometimes bitterly, when our menfolk prefer to sit by a lake or river all day rather than spend time at home helping with the household chores, but should we really mind so much?

The anglers' psyches are such that they need a certain amount of solitude, to sit quietly and contemplate, maybe philosophize a little. Then, at the end of the day, they can return home refreshed, able to cope with the trials and tribulations of life. They are much nicer people when they return from a fishing trip. Problems which, earlier in the day, made them irritable seem somehow less important after encounters with a piscatorial opponent and the knowledge, when things get too much, that they can again wander waterwards for another 'fix' of tranquillity, keeps them going for about a week.

Without these regular bouts of release there would be arguments over trivial issues, jobs around the house performed under protest and therefore badly. Physical symptoms can ensue – for both angler and his mate – migraines, raised blood pressure, odd aches and pains brought on by stress and so on.

All of this we widows can understand. What remains incomprehensible to most of us, though, is why they will give up practically anything in favour of a spot of angling. Why do they do it? What strange quirk of personality provokes the impulse to sit by a water's edge all day, or to venture on to the high seas in all weathers with one determined aim in view – to capture that which has gills?

Having enjoyed twenty-four years of marriage to an all-rounder – ie, a sea and coarse fisherman – which has included a couple of decades spent observing and attempting to analyse the behaviour of my two angling sons, several theories have sprung to mind but the real truth eludes me still. It is far too complex to consider.

We all need a certain amount of solitude in our lives. Time to sit and stare, to gather our thoughts and sort problems or ideas away, in order of importance, into our cerebral filing systems.

For we lesser mortals this can be achieved at the end of each day over a milky, bedtime drink or a small brandy. Anglers, though, seem to require longer periods to sort their lives out and use the time spent sitting at a water's edge to get things into perspective.

Maybe they have stressful and demanding jobs which leave no time for mental relaxation. Most anglers to whom I have spoken told me that, as soon as they arrive within spitting distance of water, they switch off completely from the daily grind and begin to 'think fish'. Some jobs, on the other hand, are so boring that they can be performed automatically after a while, so there is ample time for thought while at work. These anglers must go for the excitement – the buzz of adrenalin engendered by the connection with a fish to actually landing it.

I used to think, maybe naively, that there might be a sexual connotation to angling. Psychiatrists have expounded on the theory of a fishing rod being a phallic symbol, an extension of manhood, so to speak. Apparently, this is a fallacy – or should that be phallacy? – according to my Chief Angler and grown-up sons, anyway. Shame! Some of the tackle they wear, especially for sea angling, looks quite provocative to me. Still, perhaps it's just as well. We'd really have reason to be jealous if a potential co-respondent turned out to be a cod, conger eel or carp.

Why they do it isn't really the point. The fact that they do now, and will continue, way into the far distant future, is something that every woman who is contemplating alliance with an angler must take into account.

Anglers may go off on a trip with their mates but it's not a team effort. Once settled within a few feet of water they're in a world of their own. A basic instinct takes over – man against a primeval force.

Nothing short of severe incapacity will stop them, for angling becomes an obsession which, if it begins in boyhood, will endure for a lifetime. It's no good trying to blackmail, cajole or threaten. In fact, that would be the worst mistake to make, guaranteed to induce a degnerating relationship, for it would mean changing the whole personality of your partner who, we must assume, was chosen for certain aspects of his character. Take some of these aspects away and, as far as the anglers are concerned, an important part of their lives is destroyed. They become completely different people which defeats the whole object, surely?

No, anglers should not be condemned or threatened

with divorce because of their frailties. The fact that they cannot bear to be away from water for more than a week at a time is not their fault. It's a part of their make-up and therefore beyond their control.

So, lighten up all you disgruntled fishing widows. We should stick together and, let's face it, we need all the help we can get. The only way to keep sanity intact is to observe the humour in it all and it's there if you look.

Anglers regularly exhibit eccentricity so a blind eye is a necessary requirement of their womenfolk. I have become inured to the curious habits of my family, given up trying to understand it all and now accept the fact that they are slightly unbalanced. Apparently their behaviour is looked upon as normal within the fishing community – all anglers, so I'm told, act in a similar way.

Through these pages I hope to entertain and to offer reassurance. Yours are not the only anglers who perform bizarre acts at all hours of the day or night. Let me give you just one example.

I had one of these strange experiences, one evening at the end of the last coarse fishing season, when I went to pick up my eldest from the lake where he had spent the day in sub-zero temperatures hoping to tempt comatose carp. It was dark, windy, frosty cold and he was waiting for me in the car park, so I opened the boot from inside the car, ready to receive the tackle which he usually packs in first. This time, however, he flung open the passenger door, thrust carp rods past my nose and then retired to the boot area.

With the boot lid up, you can't see what's going on and he took rather longer than usual. After a few minutes the threw himself, shivering into the passenger seat – stark naked except for a pair of wet and revealing underpants and a short jacket of mine which I had foolishly left in the boot.

He had, he told me, found it necessary to jump in the lake – the times I've told him to do just that – in order to rescue a moorhen which had become entangled with someone else's irresponsibly abandoned fishing line. Stripped off, he did, in the car park, with no inhibitions whatsoever. Can't think who he gets it from. I drove home at $29\frac{1}{2}$ mph, indicated every move and smiled at passing police cars – just in case.

And on arrival in our suburban street, did he look around carefully in case there were any old biddies who might have been shocked and aghast at his state of undress? Did he heck as like! Straight out, he went, flaunting all before him, unpacked the car before I could find a door key and casually sauntered front-doorwards.

When I pointed out that it may have been a tad more sensible to strip off *before* he entered the water he had the nerve to question my lack of compassion for the poor moorhen who could have drowned in the two minutes it would have taken him to remove his clothes. I suppose he'd got a point – wasn't much left of it, though, not with a stiff north-easterly wafting around it.

This kind of odd behaviour appears to be one of the qualifications necessary to be a successful angler. Whether they are born with the genetic software already installed or whether their Bohemian outlook is acquired with practice is a question open to debate but it is definitely an integral part of the average angler's personality.

Take heart, ladies. Things can only get worse.

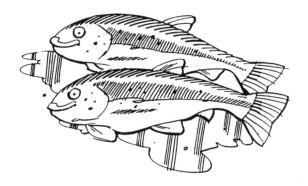

Who?

The number of people involved, directly or indirectly, in the sport of fishing amounts to millions. Ever noticed that anglers are all around us? Not just the ones we live with but the others who seem to materialize in unexpected places. I can guarantee that at any social gathering, whether we are acquainted with the other guests or not, within minutes my family have found a kindred spirit and the whole evening is interspersed with fishy anecdotes. Parties, weddings, funerals, country-pub outings – it's always the same.

Even my dentist, a charming Irishman, admits to standing thigh-deep in water with his rod pointing downstream. He has been known, he told me, to throw pretend flies at passing chub and trout, to hurl spoons and rotating silver weaponry in the general direction of confused perch or pike – and I am trusting this man with the contents of my mouth!

The half an hour he spends wrist deep is accompanied by a non-stop monologue about venues, baits, lures etc. I'm a captive audience, can't answer back – and he knows it.

He approaches menacingly with the drill and tells of the terror experienced as the shingle moves underfoot and the current tries to sweep him away before he has caught anything. He gave me the impression that if he had been swept away and drowned *after* he had caught something it wouldn't have mattered so much – and I could certainly relate to his terror as I kept an eye on the flight path of that drill.

Then there was the gas fitter who arrived in four feet of snow to fix the central heating. We had been without heat or hot water for two days and it was so cold that our boys had stopped arguing and sat, huddled together under a duvet, with the fiftieth cup of soup-of-the-day to warm them up. Did he get stuck in to the errant boiler? The fishing-rod rack is just inside the front door. What d'you think?

There followed a twenty-minute discussion with the Chief Angler on the merits of carbon-fibre against split cane and thereafter, frequent five minute 'rests' to evaluate boilies versus bread/luncheon meat for capturing carp.

Eventually the gas man borrowed one of my knitting needles and poked it about in the outside pipes to de-ice them. The boiler sprang into life and the house began to warm up but for half a day the discussions were more heated than the radiators.

I've been reduced to tears of tedium by the baker, from whom I have to purchase freshly baked half an hour ago, farmhouse loaves for my Chief Angler to throw, in succulent chunks, into a lake. I once made the mistake of telling the baker that it mattered not if the bread was yesterday's, it was only for fishing – he has never let me forget it.

Years ago, when called upon by my son's form tutor to discuss his future – guess the subject most under discussion. My son's hobbies and interests were seriously looked into. The one interest/hobby was given undivided attention, experiences narrated, photographs exchanged and Dave emerged from the meeting having been put down several groups in French but in charge of the Aquarium Club and captain of the school's fishing squad.

After persuading my Chief Angler that we desperately needed an 'ex-display, going cheap' kitchen, I had to coax him into the showroom. He was reluctant to sign the agreement until, by a chance remark, we discovered that the proprietor of the kitchen firm is an angler. My CA signed the forms almost absentmindedly while carrying on a conversation about a local match – due to take place the following weekend.

Then there are the ones who are involved in selling equipment, bait and so on. You should make the effort to get to know your local tackle dealer for, whether you like it or not, you will need to ask his advice on many occasions.

Garbled telephone conversations with your anglers will reveal that they have manipulated a day off work tomorrow, and intend to leave for a reasonable-sized volume of water at 4 am the following morning.

'You'd better write this down,' they'll say kindly, making patronizing allowance for your ignorance. 'And then go round to Cliff's. Ask him for a pint of mixed, a packet of rubbers, a waggler, a spoon and six Arsley bombs.'

Do you think it sounds more like a job for the chemist? Have you any idea what it all means? No, neither have I, but Cliff knows, so you should be nice to him at all times, you never know when you may need his help in a hurry.

Your local tackle shop is full to overflowing with a

myriad of items for the serious and dedicated angler, ranging from a 40p float to a roach pole which could set them back about £1,500. There are degrees of dedication.

There are objects on open shelves that conjure up all kinds of visions – some bewildering and others downright frightening. What about the 'Deep-Throat' disgorger? I personally don't like the sound of that one. Then there are 'Carp Ears' which I'm told are only extensions for bite-alarms – the carp haven't been mutilated – and how about a 'Twitcher Wheel'? What on earth could that be for? It sounds like a treadmill for hamsters – maybe for anglers who can't relax and need to keep moving while waiting for the action.

A sliding rod-pod aerial sounds interesting – it's for the monkey climber apparently – whatever *that* means. He even stocks a Bivvy Peg Extractor for those anglers who want to conserve their energies for better things than taking the pegs out of tents at the end of the day. All this information is subliminally ingested on the way to the counter, from which it is best to avert your eyes on approach – unless you can tolerate several million maggots, of varying hues, struggling for supremacy in the half-dozen or so temptingly displayed trays.

There will be one group of experienced anglers in the shop at any one time – who will view you askance as you walk in clutching your script and snigger quietly as you confidently read from it the items desperately needed for tomorrow. They know you haven't a clue what you are talking about but to hand over the paper with the money wrapped in it makes you feel too much like a small child on an errand for Mummy, so only do this as a last resort.

Fortunately Cliff knows from experience exactly

what is needed. He will ask you a couple of probing questions – 'What's he going for? Tench or pike?' or 'Where's he off to? Carp lake or river?' – then miraculously transform your faltering mispronunciation into items of tackle.

Sometimes it is possible just to mention the size and type of hook required. Your tackle dealer will be able to tell you where they are going, what they are hoping to catch and what time they'll be home for their tea – although I don't think even a clairvoyant could foretell that, the anglers themselves can never come up with a sensible answer when asked – but the tackle dealer certainly seems to possess powers beyond the understanding of a mere fishing widow.

Most tackle shops are like a club house. Coffee is served to the regulars and the owner offers words of wisdom and comfort when tragedy strikes – eg, broken rods or drowned equipment. He repairs their fractured reels with almost fanatical devotion and makes up that special rod to their own specifications, rejoicing with them in their conquests. When he is in the shop, that is, for tackle dealers are usually anglers too and often feel the need to delegate the responsibility of trading to a trusted colleague while they sneak off for a few hours.

When your anglers tell you that they are 'Just going up to Cliff's. Won't be a minute. Got to get a couple of swivels for tomorrow,' you can bet on an hour at least before they return, refreshed and invigorated from a mug of coffee and a chat.

Christmas and birthdays need no longer be a headache if you have a good relationship with your tackle dealer. Presents abound and he already knows, down to the nearest hook, what your anglers have already, so it is relatively easy for him to suggest something new. It beats wandering around the shops searching for shirts or socks, anyway, and you can be sure that your gift will be received with genuine appreciation. Far more satisfying than a noncommittal 'That's nice,' when you offer a new pair of slippers.

Tackle dealers generally are long-suffering and one of the vital ingredients which make up a happy angling household. Where would we fishing widows be without them?

What?

Anglers, to the uneducated general public, are lumped together in one simple category. The reality is totally the opposite. There is a world of difference between a sea angler who goes for conger eel, cod, skate or bass and a dedicated coarse fisherman who sits for hours on a river bank trying to ensnare roach, rudd or perch. The fresh-water brigade should be divided into specialist compartments too for there are those who only go to catch pike, or barbel or carp.

Every species of fish has its own dietary preferences, so the study of baits can become a science and if you are partner to a man who will have a go at catching anything, then it is prudent to invest in a separate fridge/freezer solely for the purpose of storing diverse bait components.

Maggots as bait are legendary. They have been used, along with various types of worm, for centuries and are a basic necessity for every coarse angler. They cannot be frozen for the obvious reason that, once dead through frostbite, their potential as a live, wriggling thing on the end of a hook is lost for ever. They must be kept alive at the expense of your salad tray.

Complaining about maggots in the fridge, girls? Think yourself lucky that they are where you can see 'em. The alternative is too awful to contemplate. If they are stored elsewhere, lids can become loose and the little devils wriggle into inaccessible places.

Three weeks after being let loose in the house they metamorphose into the most laid-back bluebottles in the universe. Almost Jamaican in attitude – and that's not intended as a derogatory, racist description, believe me. I have the utmost respect and admiration for the West Indian culture which allows its people to take life as it comes. These bluebottles, bred in captivity, are big, relaxed and unruffled. As they fly lethargically low, hoping to find an open window, you almost expect them to ask about the cricket score as they drone past your nose, like miniature Lancaster bombers, towards freedom.

Still, when all is said and done, a maggot is a maggot, isn't it? Well, no, not really. Not according to my local tackle-shop dealer, it isn't. They come in various guises. Fluorescent reds, plain reds, squats – that means little ones, I was told on inquiry – plain, white or fluorescent. Pinkies, casters, on and on *ad nauseum*. At least, that's how I felt by the time I had been shown the menu – all in glorious technicolour – and I'd only shown a polite interest!

There doesn't appear to be any particular reason for the difference in colour, apparently it's a matter of personal preference. Anglers wax lyrical over these repulsive little creatures but, don't be misled, they all finish up as the same colour bluebottles.

Then there are boilies. Carp love these small orbs of succulence, home-made or mass produced and flavoured with pungent oils of fruit, fish or meat. They should cause the average fishing widow very little in the way of lost sleep, you may think.

It depends where you find them. Those which are hastily decanted from frozen packets into small pots, as your anglers try to escape as quickly as possible in the early hours of the morning, can roll away and hide in secret corners or under bookcases, to be discovered eventually by the vacuum cleaner, by which time they have become rock solid balls of concrete and will do the innards of your domestic appliance no good at all.

Baits used for sea angling need far more care and attention than the fresh-water ones. Rag/lugworms are dug up, with monotonous regularity, during the winter months and are brought home in a large bucket which is dumped, in the centre of a clean kitchen carpet, while a mountain of old newspaper, kept expressly for this exercise, is retrieved from under the stairs.

It is always too windy, raining or cold in the garden to execute the painstaking job of wrapping all the worms in newsprint – carefully, one them must not touch another – so the whole operation is carried out on the kitchen floor. The ensuing worm juice stains which seep through the paper on to the carpet are easily removed with a little 1001 and a lot more elbow grease.

Crabs, soft-backed and vulnerable, should be contained at all costs, preferably in something which has a lid. Otherwise they try, with surprising success, to escape by standing on each others' backs until they reach the bucket rim. There are always a few truants scuttling aimlessly up and down the hallway if a lidless bucket is left by the front door overnight. And speaking of crabs, there are other hazards to be recognized, apart from tripping over one or two in the dark.

My Chief Angler is a commercial artist and it's a job which involves working unsocial hours. At least, that's what he says – they sound pretty sociable to me, evey time he rings me it seems to be from a pub.

A few years back I received a distraught phone call from the studio where he was desperately trying to meet a deadline. He had been out on the mud, nearly all of the previous Saturday, harvesting crabs intended for bait on the Sunday. About a hundred of the blessed creatures fell to this onslaught but the weather took a turn for the worse just hours before the charter-boat was due to leave the wharf so, inevitably, the crabs were duly brought home and placed lovingly into a large photographic tray, about three feet square, which stood expectantly in the shed. Hubby 'borrowed' the aerator pump from the kids' fish tank – the fish had to be content with those fizzy tablets said to provide oxygen for a week or two, the crabs were far more important – and satisfied that his bounty would be safe until the following Sunday, he went about his usual business.

This phone call was a plea for clemency. Could I? Would I please go into the shed and examine his friends? 'Just pick out the dead ones,' he pleaded. 'And move the others about a bit. Ring me back and let me know if they're all right.'

I opened the shed door to be greeted by silence. Hardly any movement at all but, as I approached the tray, a couple of the braver ones waved at me so I knew I'd have to go through with it. I deduced, because I'm not completely stupid, that the ones that didn't move at all were dead. Others who only moved when I poked them were not feeling very well and the ones who ran about a lot were going to make it. I also knew, that if I put my hand in that tray, in order to remove the dead ones, their brethren would try to bite my fingers off. Well, wouldn't you? If I was a crab I'd certainly try and exact some kind of revenge. They were not to know that mine was not the same hand that had cruelly plucked them from their natural habitat to live in a tray.

A slotted spoon was the answer, together with a couple of Pyrex bowls – one to receive the corpses, the other to segregate the terminally ill ones. It took me three-quarters of an hour to complete this errand of mercy and when I rang back the anxious one, he had the cheek to ask me to pay a visit to the children's paddling pool to obtain fresh seawater and a mite of seaweed – just enough to rejuvenate them.

I went, of course. These pools, situated at intervals along our foreshore, consist of large, shallow walls – square-shaped and made of concrete – which hold back some of the tide when it goes out. Gives the kids somewhere to fill up their buckets before hurling the contents over Grandma's feet. Trying to drive home without spilling a bucket of seawater in the boot is no easy task, let me tell you. Had I not taken all the corners at five miles an hour it could have given a whole, new meaning to a 'boot sail'.

The above method of crab preservation is a marginal improvement on the other one commonly used by heartless sea anglers. Live crabs, surplus to immediate requirements, are sometimes frozen alive, without a chloroform pad to ease their passing. It is evident that they suffer greatly for if you look into their Tupperware box the following day you will notice that, in their death throes, they have all huddled together for warmth in one corner.

The callousness of anglers takes some getting used to and can be quite disturbing to a new fishing widow, especially if the angler is kind and compassionate in all other aspects of his life. It comes as a shock to observe how they treat the lesser species of nature and it is useless to protest, for all they will say is 'Ever heard a fish/worm/crab say "ouch"?'

All is not lost, however, for I'm sure that our anglers must have the occasional pangs of conscience – there's no other explanation for the inevitable leglessness in the pub after every fishing trip.

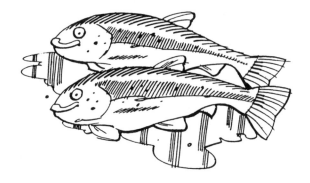

When?

There are hundreds of books and magazines about all aspects of fishing and we've all read a few, although not through choice. The subject matter is left lying about on the floor of the loo and it seems to be a natural reflex to pick it up and read while being otherwise engaged.

These publications tell mostly of where to look for record specimens. Which baits to use to lure the poor creatures to their doom. Where to catch what. How to tie knots or to avoid bird's nests. The techniques of caring for soft-backed crabs all week so that they can be hurled great distances at the weekend and how to mix up the most disgusting messes, euphemistically called 'rubby-dubby', which are guaranteed to force any self-respecting fish to give itself up. All this and more, but no one tells us how to cope with living from day to day in a fishing household and at the same time hang on to our sanity.

You will have to cook some of the results of their sea-angling trips. The respectable, professionally written books on fish cookery are great if your big white hunters bring home hake, turbot or smoked haddock but, as every angler's woman knows, the more usual offering is a hurriedly filleted cod before the pub opens, or a few dabs which they've left whole because the resulting fillets would be about two inches square.

And what about the competition fish? I mean the ones that have lain naked on the deck all day with their innards in instead of out because every gram counts at the weigh-in? By the time you get them it's very nearly too late. There is never advice about how to disguise them and make them edible, or more importantly, how to avoid the eventual use of alcohol or tranquillizers after a few months/years of wedded bliss to an angler.

I feel sorry for the newly married fishing widows. No one has tried to tell them how to cope with live crabs or wriggling creatures in the salad tray, how to get rid of the stubborn ring of mud and other things that appear at every bathtime, or the removal of best part of the foreshore to be regularly trodden in to carpets. Someone should, for they need sympathy and understanding and after a while, probably the Samaritans.

Some of the answers to the dilemmas facing FWs only come after years of experience and in some cases not even then. Many of us are experienced but perplexed – in fact some FWs have been known to become so perplexed that they file for divorce, but this is an extreme measure and with the right approach should not be necessary.

One of the most important aspects of fishing widowhood is to get accustomed to the fact that your year will still be made up of 'the seasons' – but rather more than the usual four.

As far as sea angling is concerned, each season varies in length depending on how many fish of the same species are caught in any time span – and some seasons overlap. All a bit confusing, especially as the 'seasons'

vary from year to year – depending on climatic con-
ditons.

The seasons in my angling household are like this –
yours may vary:

Skate: skate is caught for a short season in the summer.
Short because it is generally too windy at the weekends
for the charter-boat to leave the wharf. Monday to
Friday the sun shines and we have to cancel the kite
flying trips but on the skate-hunting weekend a howling gale springs up at midnight Friday and eventually
dies down late on Sunday afternoon.

When skate does get brought home, therefore, you
must first stand about muttering words of praise and
admiration and then promptly do something pretty
good with it, otherwise the menfolk will assume that
their efforts are unappreciated and will give the next
catch away to their mates.

Eels: these have an even shorter season than skate
because they are not allowed past the front door. Eels
should be given to your grandmother who will chop
them up and hurl them into the nearest hot frying pan
containing a soupçon of dripping, salt and pepper.
When they have stopped moving of their own accord,
she will eat them all and ask for more. They can also be
stewed gently in a little salted water with a handful of
parsley and allowed to cool when they will jelly nastily
and be pronounced delicious. Elderly gentlemen in
fishing villages smoke eels but then they'll smoke
anything if it fits into a pipe.

Bass: bass must be accompanied by champagne and
much touching of the forelock to the fortunate captor.
They are caught in high summer when the last thing
you need is to be cooped up in a hot kitchen playing
with food.

Flounders: usually offered to their womenfolk by

junior anglers and for obvious reasons must be received with suitable awe and reconstructed into something edible. As these little gifts of love are usually minuscule the only possible way to cook them, without losing various parts of your anatomy during the filleting process, is to cook them whole.

If you use plenty of garlic, parsley and salt, and fry them gently in butter, the God-awful muddy taste of these creatures will not seep through on to your plate. Yes, *you* will have to eat them too and probably on being seen to enjoy them so much, will be forcibly offered the leftovers from junior plates. Claiming a tummy ache brought on by a surfeit of flounders will not be accepted as an excuse not to clean up the lot.

24

Dab and Sole: I had the great honour once, and only once, of being taken out on a charter-boat to receive angling instruction. I caught a sole by mistake though I had no intention of catching anything except the sun. While I was making friends with a couple of crabs, whom I had named the Kray twins and which my newly wed husband, the kindest and gentlest of men, eventually ripped the legs off and threw over the side with a hook rammed in their poor little bellies, a sole of some proportion somehow attached itself to my line and when I reeled it in half an hour later – there it was.

The disapproval of the other members of the party, for up until then no one else had caught anything, was enough to deter me from ever going again. The fact that I was never again invited is beside the point.

Cod: a smart woman can always spot the advent of the cod season. Anxious glances at the garden thermometer and the involuntary switching of TV channels in order to catch all the weather forecasts at once gives it away. Tights disappear from knicker drawers, only to resurrect themselves, totally mutilated, some days later in the washing basket. I refuse to hang these articles outside to dry with their neat, razor-bladed 'fly' cut in the front. Polythene bags are discovered, sweaty and disgusting inside wellington boots – and try to find a woolly hat when you want one that isn't covered in ragworm juice and/or fish scales.

There is raucous male laughter and a smell of cigar smoke from downstairs at 4 am when the lads have been brought home for coffee when the weather is too inclement to venture out on the high seas. They eventually depart with much ssh'ing and giggling around 6.30 am after which their host will bound upstairs, jump into bed freezing coold and smelling strongly of seawater, demanding to know why you are not remotely turned on by his presence.

The benefits of these minor inconveniences are few except for the million and one ways in which you can disguise cod when they do catch some.

Whiting: a whiting infestation usually precedes the influx of cod fillets. They are reputed to be of a very delicate flavour but, in my opinion, they are so delicate as to be virtually tasteless and my family lean towards food that blows their heads off. So, I make fish cakes with whiting and serve them with a tomato and garlic sauce. It's the only way to get rid of the blessed things.

Tidal time capsules pale into insignificance compared to the fresh-water season. This now spans all year too and, if you choose a coarse angler for your mate, you will be left alone for long periods as he heads for the river or lake regardless of the time of day – or night – and the weather conditions. Carp anglers camp out for days at a time which involves the transportation of mountains of gear and enough food to feed a regiment. One of the few advantages to FWs is the fact that coarse anglers cook their own food at the water's edge and they don't bring their catch home but return it carefully to the lake, which is just as well because the culinary value of most fresh-water species is negligible.

Take heart. You can cope. It's just a matter of being one jump ahead of the game. Life can be fun with an angler – if you let it.

Where?

Anywhere! Any small dot of inland blue. Lakes, rivers or chalk streams. Any pool, puddle or trickling rill. A rugged coastline, piers, jetties, a windswept beach – and they always are when applied to fishing.

Beach competitons are usually held in adverse weather conditions which slowly deteriorate even further as the day progresses. By about lunchtime, when the wind has reached thirty knots and there is hail mixed in with the rain, you may decide to jump into the car and go and see if they are all right. This is a common mistake made by FWs especially if Junior Anglers are involved.

On arrival at the appropriate pegs, and this is not as easy as it sounds because the pegs stretch for five miles along the shore and your anglers could be anywhere, you'll find that your eldest son has eaten everything that hasn't moved within a hundred-yard radius, is starving to death, has developed frostbite, probably hypothermia and will collapse into a coma in about twenty minutes unless you can rush home and make it back in time, clutching a Thermos of hot soup, a dozen or so corned-beef sandwiches and a Black Forest gateau.

He has also forgotten to take along his hat and gloves but another sweater would make his life almost bearable, so you lend him yours because you don't want him home from school with double pneumonia and incessantly chattering about angling technique. It's only a mile and a half walk to where you parked the car and then you will be warm again. It seems like the London Marathon.

Hubby will have totally ignored your presence even though he is only two pegs away. He is concentrating.

Fishing Boat Festivals can continue for two days at a time with a brief respite of a few hours' sleep. Not for you; your anglers will be so possessed that even when asleep they'll mutter about paternoster rigs, rubby-dubby and only needing one big one to clinch the match. You will deal with today's bucket of fish, left triumphantly on the draining board, and will sleep when they have ventured out onto the high seas again at 4 am.

By the time the match is over on Sunday evening, they are totally exhausted. The weigh-in takes hours and tempers become frayed as alcohol begins to affect their already haggard features and jet-lagged intellects so there are low-voiced accusations of cheating, forged aggregate papers, dodgy scales and stewards with a bias.

The fish, duly weighed and documented, remain in their assorted containers, slowly decaying in the heat of two hundred bodies and the accumulated fumes of blood, sweat, tears and alcohol, until the officials have reached a verdict, when the fish may be disposed of.

Then begins the interminable prizegiving which seems to involve an exorbitant number of categories: heaviest round fish, runner-up to heaviest round fish, heaviest flat fish, runner-up, heaviest mixed bag, runner-up, top weight, runner-up, greatest number of fish, runner-up and more.

The prizes are presented for charter-boats, private boats, juniors and ladies so you have to go through the whole procedure four times. Oh yes, then there is the skipper's prize. He is now the proud owner of yet another wine decanter or coffee-making machine – he has fifteen of each at home already.

During the above proceedings, ie, post weigh-in and pre prizegiving, the experienced FW will persuade or threaten her angler into leaving the alcoholic haze for an invigorating breeze on the beach in order to decapitate and evacuate the stomachs of his catch, and possibly his own for by now the fish are almost putrid.

With the fish already loaded into the boot, all that needs to be done at the end of the day is to steer the menfolk in the direction of the car park. They will expect a hot, three-course meal to be ready and waiting when they get home. Chinese restaurants stay open quite late.

Very occasionally the prizegiving ritual is thinly dis-guised as a dinner and dance. It is the one night a year that fishing widows can wear a decent frock but it's a rare occurrence. Nevertheless, all competitions are an integral part of a FW's life and must be treated with respect for it's no use telling your anglers that it's only a game – they won't believe you.

The fresh-water venues are far more pleasant places to be, if you are able to relax without feeling guilty. Quite often you will find yourself at the same lake and beside the same swim as the previous weekend but, if you take the time to look around you, you will find that everything is different.

Every time we visit our local lakes there is a diverse element to it all. I only go in the summer months so the weather is usually hot and overcast, maybe sultry with a hint of a thunderstorm later. I make them put the bivvie up first, before they set up the rods. Just for me and just in case. It is possible, sometimes preferable, to let your mind wander and just observe.

Two grebes are lazily circling the lake, and each other, meeting every thirty seconds for a kiss and whispered secret or two. The tufts on their heads nodding like a couple of elderly ladies on a park bench reminiscing about the old days. A pair of majestic swans glide by. Galleons in full sail, they are closely followed by only two cygnets. Where are the others, I wonder? There are usually more than two.

I'm sure the population of ducks, coots and moorhens has increased since we were last here, or maybe they are concentrated within our view because of the amount of weed on the lake today – that has definitely increased. The coots are stabbing through the weed with their beaks, after grubs and the multitude of storm flies that seem to be everywhere.

There are wood pigeons cooing in the oak tree beneath which I made them pitch the bivvie. A contrapuntal duet with quite an interesting rhythm which is going to distract when the time comes for me to retire inside with a library book. Maybe the storm will hold off. Maybe I'll just hide in it for a while this afternoon, to gain a respite from the wasps and mosquitoes which seem to home in on my yellow hair. It's too hot to wear a hat.

A song thrush is singing its heart out in an adjacent tree, its breast proud and speckled, full to the brim and spilling over with melody. Black-headed gulls are screaming overhead, they've ventured inland from the salt marshes a few miles to the south of us, always the sign of a storm when the gulls come in.

Across the lake a group of anglers are standing, seemingly carefully posed and completely motionless. They could be an eighteenth-century oil painting with birch, elder and willow casting mirror images on the silver, eau-de-nil opalescence of the water in the foreground.

Time to go for a walk, I think. My anglers are settled and waiting, although the weed plays tricks on them. It's pretty bad on the lake today, they have had to turn down the sensitivity on the bite-alarms, not that it makes much difference. A coot scooted past just now, paddling a lump of weed over the lines. The bite-alarms went crazy and everyone made a dive for their rod – it's quite difficult to know when to strike and when to ignore. They will sort it out sooner or later. Plenty of bubbles on the top of the water though, rising up through the weed – that means the carp are in there somewhere.

A couple of hours have elapsed and several cups of coffee have begun to make themselves felt. Definitely time to go for a walk. I wander slowly in the direction of the little wooden hut, laughingly called a toilet but better than nothing, taking a plastic bag with me so I can gather a handful of blackberries on the way back. If I visit the wooden hut often enough there will be sufficient blackberries for a pie by the end of the afternoon.

They all wondered why I came back grinning after my first visit of the day. I told them why. Inside, taped to the wall was a scrap of white paper, about three inches square. On it was drawn a graphic cartoon of a beer advertisement spider, with an arrow pointing towards a far corner of the wooden hut – the legend inscribed underneath it read 'I bet *he* drinks Carling Black Label.' I found myself looking for the imaginary spider – I bet other folk did too.

Dog daisies which, years ago, grew abundantly on bomb sites and the musty scent of the elderberry bushes make me think of my grandmother. She used to make elderberry wine and dish it out to me when I was a child, on Sundays after church. I can still remember the warmth of it in my throat, the pungent taste of elderberry and the crystal clear glasses in which she served it. She made sloe gin too but it was several years before I discovered exactly what this was. I naively imagined it to be a drink that she sipped very slowly.

After spending some time with my grandfather and fortified by the wine we would walk the half mile to my home, taking a stroll through the rose gardens of a local park on the way. There was an ornamental pond in this park, only about ten or twelve feet square. It contained several carp and I remember them as being huge – they probably weren't but everything looks larger or better in retrospect, especially nostalgic memories from childhood. Grandfather would eventually have to disturb these creatures with his walking stick, from where they lay hidden under the lily-pads, because I refused to move on before catching a glimpse of at least one of them on the move. They've all gone now, grandparents and carp. Some years ago, borough officialdom with no soul turned the gardens, including the pond, into a children's playground, asphalt and all. They called it progress.

Mid afternoon and not so much as a knock on any of the six rods. A bite-alarm screams from half a dozen swims away and all my anglers list to the left in an effort to see the result – at least they know the carp are biting despite the weed. The fortunate angler lands a ten-pound common, gives his audience a thumbs-up sign and the excitement is over.

By teatime the youngest has given up trying to tempt unco-operative carp and begins to float fish into a few inches of clear water close to the lake edge. He has had the forethought to bring along a few maggots and has some success with baby tench which are smaller than the occasional roach taking his bait. He has left one rod out for carp though, you never know.

Four geese are flying overhead, speeding by in strict formation and honking in careful harmony, like a barber's shop quartet. I wish I knew where they were going.

There is a muted bleep from one of our bite-alarms, a strike and a bent rod – until the fish hits the weed bed when the reel groans and spits. Husband curses as line falls off the spool in grey clouds and the fish escapes into the reeds. Another little job when we get home, trying to discover the source of the malfunction. Luckily the youngest has a spare reel – always prepared, the youngest.

Dusk isn't far off now. We will stay until the last possible moment. The great escape has put new heart into my anglers and it becomes like the final minute before the referee's whistle – but they won't win today. It doesn't seem to matter. They are quite cheerful as they pack everything away until next time and we hurry towards the car park. The clouds have thickened, there is a distant rumble of thunder and a few spots of rain lightly caress our faces. Maybe we'll reach home before the storm breaks.

This and That

An Angler's Wife's Lament

There's boilies in the bathroom,
There's crabs loose in the shed
And maggots in the salad tray,
There's swivels on the bed.
There's rods and reels in every room,
Step over, if you please,
The oil-skins, romper suits and gloves,
Deep almost to your knees.
The house is like a tackle shop,
Full to the brim with gear,
And all to catch the massive carp,
Or mackerel off the pier.

The man who fishes in the lakes,
His son prefers the sea,
They fish 'em turn and turn about,
It makes no sense to me.
We cook their food and wash their clothes,
For the smell of fishing lingers,

They put the tench back in the lake,
So we must buy fish fingers.

Why is it that the angling bug
Bites deep and grips so tight?
And what would happen to you all
If the fish refused to bite?
You'd have to stay at home a lot
And would we wives be glad?
Of course not, for your fishing tales
Would drive us raving mad.

The Angler's Ode

The greatest love of all my life
Apart from children (and the wife)
Is fishing in the seas and lakes,
I'm easy pleased, that's all it takes.
To keep me sane and satisfied,
Feel like a man and boost my pride,
I need to find what's in the deep.
I even fish when I'm asleep.

I think about it every day.
I never hear what people say
Unless they speak of rod or reel
Or call me for another meal.
I know I should be more at home
With those who care, and never roam,
But it's so hard to stay inside,
Ignore the calling of the tide.

I have to go down to the sea,
I take some mates along with me,

We laugh and joke and catch the fish.
It never ends, that's all I wish.
The lakes and rivers soothe my soul,
Carp, roach, or barbel are my goal,
And while I wait for float to sink
It gives me time to sit and think.

My life's serene, without a quirk,
For other people do the work.
I do not dig nor wield a brush,
Nor round a supermarket rush.
My spare time's taken up, you see,
With the one thing that interests me,
Fishing comes first, it always will,
'Cos I can never get my fill.

If everybody thought like me,
The world a different place would be,
There'd be no wars. The bomb? They'd ban it,
And not a fish left on the planet.
I dream of places far away,
Where I could sit and fish all day,
Who knows? I might catch more than cold,
The big one's more to me than gold.

One day I'll beat the record, mate,
And all I have to do is wait,
The day will come, of that I'm sure,
But until then I'll fish some more.
When I grow grey and far too old
To go out fishing in the cold,
What will I do? Sit in the sun
And tell the youngsters how it's done.

Rhymes of Ancient Mariners

Sea Fever

(Let's hope John Masefield never finds out)

I must go down to the sea again, to the lonely sea and
the sky,
And all I ask is a bucket of bait, don't know the reason
why.
And the wind's soft, and the air's calm, and the ebb tide
beckons,
We're sure to catch a big'un today, or so the skipper
reckons.

I must go down to the sea again, for the call of the run-
ning tide,
Is a wild call and a clear call, and may not be denied.
And all I ask is a boat-rod, with the fish all biting,
And the reel spin, and the line tight, and an occasional
school of whiting.

I must go down to the seas again, with the mates I hold
so dear,
While the cod wait, and the cans fizz, when they open
another beer.
And all I ask is a huge fish, I only want but one.
And quiet sleep and a sweet dream, when the long
trip's done.

Ancient Superstitions

Never say 'rabbits' aboard our boat,
It causes the skipper pain.
He won't care, if you're half way there,
He'll bring you straight home again.

Don't whistle at sea, at any price,
It makes the wind blow stronger,
A force eight gale springs up in a trice,
And you can 'whistle' for your conger.

If a falling star you see,
Back to harbour, as soon as may be,
For though the night be calm, and warm,
A falling star foretells a storm.

Eat mackerel and herring from tail to head,
Or fish flee the fishing grounds, so 'tis said.

When the wind's in the north, the fish come forth.
When the wind's in the east, the fish bite least.
When the wind's in the west, the fish bit best.
When the wind's in the south, they take nothing by
    mouth.

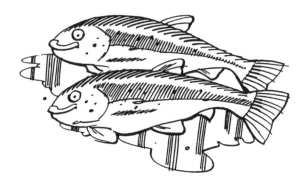

The Fishing Widow's Clinic

From Instant Salmonella, of Southsea

My live-in boyfriend keeps putting live soft-backed crabs in the salad tray in our fridge. He doesn't even bother to remove the lettuce and spring onions first but says that the fumes from the onions keep the crabs conscious and the lettuce acts as surrogate seaweed. What can I do?

Dear Instant,

Wait until your boyfriend has gone to the pub and then turn up the thermostat in the fridge. Turn this down half an hour before the pubs close. The crabs will no longer be soft-backed but hard and crunchy, thus totally decimating his bait supply. Unless he is a complete cretin, this should deter him from repeating the exercise.

From Airborne Disaster Area of Luton

There are dozens of bluebottles flying about in my

bedroom and my husband says that they must have come from my knicker drawer. I know this cannot be true but every time I manage to get rid of them another lot seem to appear about three weeks later. Help.

Dear Airborne,

Keep your knickers in the AIRing cupboard and tell him to keep his maggots to himself.

From Hooked, of Holland

I think we have a poltergeist in the house. I go shopping once a week and stock up the store cupboard but tins of sweetcorn and luncheon meat seem to disappear overnight and no one knows where they have gone. Should I call in a priest?

Dear Hooked,

Your groceries are being thrown in a river. The only course of action is to hit your husband on the head with a priest. He is bound to have at least one in his tackle box.

From Nervous Wreck, of 25 miles out from Brixham, Devon

I spend a lot of my time waiting at the harbour for the fishing boats to come in. Sometimes I have to wait a long time and I have been approached by strange men in the dark. How can I cope with this?

Dear Nervous,

These men are harmless. They are bemused anglers and

all they want from you is that you wash their wader's socks. Carry a packet of washing powder, point out that you are waiting for a particular angler and they will leave you alone.

From Floundering, of Finland

I have to shampoo my carpets at least once a week to remove stains of mud, oil, tar, fish juices, lager and spilt curry sauce from takeaways. This is wearing the carpets out and I cannot afford to keep replacing them. What shall I do?

Dear Floundering,

Replace your carpets for the last time but choose the colour carefully. A mixture of black/brown/grey and orange is ideal. If you avoid spills of blackcurrant juice no one will ever know the difference. On no account allow anyone to bleed on the carpet otherwise all your efforts will have been in vain.

From Codpiece, of Cornwall

I am sure that my husband is having an affair with two other women. He talks in his sleep and always speaks passionately about Eb and Flo. I'm so afraid he is going to leave me.

Dear Codpiece,

Don't worry. Your husband's problem is tidal and he will only leave you for twelve-hourly stints at sea. When he mutters in his sleep, just whisper in his ear things like 'The wind's dropped' or 'The tide's not in yet.' This should put his mind at rest and you'll both get a good night's sleep.

And finally – from shell-shocked, of Southampton

My husband and three sons keep using the 'f' word. It appears in their conversation in almost every other sentence and when I protest, they argue that it is heard everywhere nowadays – even on TV. I find it most upsetting. How can I stop them saying it?

Dear Shocked,

You will never be able to stop them from saying it. Try to ignore it. I understand your concern but the word 'fishing' comes from the old Anglo-Saxon and is becoming quite acceptable in polite society.

PART TWO

The Carp Widow

Life at the Lake

You may spend a great deal of your leisure time at a lake – if you wish to enjoy the company of your family, that is – for once the carp bug bites they'll be there at every waking, non-working moment and the only way you will ever see them is if you tag along.

The preparation for carp fishing seems to be never ending, the most time-consuming activity being the side issue of bait production. Boilies are purchased or home-made then steeped in various foul-smelling oils. Even the sweet, exotic, fruit-flavoured oil will over-power the fumes from a garlic-infested curry that is stewing gently on the hob – and the pungent fish varieties really knock you back. I have a friend who is afraid to open the cupboard where the oils are stored – the emanation is such that it seems as if something tangible will jump out at you but, strangely, the carp seem to enjoy food containing these heady essences. It makes me wonder what on earth they eat when boilies are not being hurled into their environment.

These 1,000-times concentrated oils, of any flavour, pose a threat to fishing widows. They permeate everything that the anglers touch and are almost impossible to get rid of. Clothes need at least three sessions on the heavy soil cycle of the washing machine and even then there is still a faint aroma of unpleasantness.

The people who make the advert on TV for a washing powder that banishes dirt *and* smells obviously haven't heard of boilie oil, maybe someone should challenge them. And another word of warning. Do not, no matter how much of a hurry you may be in, borrow your anglers' polaroids. The frantic application of a bar of Camay, plus a whole bottle of perfume, barely disguises the smell left on your face and you will get very odd glances from people who pass you in the street.

Anglers will spend hours making up traces at home which, they say, necessitates the contents of tackle boxes being spread all over the best Wilton. And if they run out of Superglue, used to make sure the traces hold up under pressure, at 9 pm on a Saturday evening it means 'someone' will have to undertake a ten-mile drive to the nearest all-night garage to get this vital ingredient.

Carp anglers are obsessive and suffer cold turkey whenever anything thwarts their desire to head for the carp lake. The angler who belongs to the fishing widow with the terrifying cupboard recently underwent a very serious back operation. He lay there like a petulant child.

Is he in pain? Yes, a bit. Is he so depressed because he is forced to lie flat on his back for three weeks? Not really, although he is slightly fed up with the inactivity. What can it be then? What terrible trauma is he experiencing that is causing such despair and obvious distress?

He can't get to the lake. He has read every angling publication on earth at least twice. He can smell the

boilies beckoning from the *Halloween II* cupboard and, as soon as he can stagger to his feet again, he will throw himself under a bus – such is his misery. Never mind the fact that he is fortunate that he will be able to walk at all – he wants to go carping *now*! We go to the lake regularly but dare not tell him if anything over twenty pounds is caught – we want him to go on living.

Severe withdrawal symptoms are not pleasant to witness so every attempt should be made to prevent them. Suffering a day out lakeside is far preferable to trying to alleviate your deprived anglers' suffering as they mope about at home.

On arrival at the lake car park you will be told that you 'only have to carry the food and your blanket'. These items weigh sixteen tons. Try carrying four bottles of mineral water, a large flask of coffee and a squillion sandwiches for half a mile or so. Just as your arms are about to drop off, your anglers will stop and gaze about them, looking for the best swim near which to set up camp for the day. They'll decide on a decent place, unpack all the gear and then realize that there's a better area 'just round the next bend'.

'There are too many people here,' your Chief Angler will complain. He doesn't mean too many anglers, just too many mums, grandmothers and small children, but before long they settle down and you can start reading your book.

The carp seem to have a similar mentality to their captors. For three hours the swims have been baited. The rods have been tackled up and pointed, virginal but expectant, towards the visible carp who are busy playing leapfrog over by the reeds. Now is the time during the lull, you may think, to feed your family.

Don't you believe it. The carp wait until you have

unwrapped all the sandwiches and poured the coffee then they will immediately grab a hook each and you have chaos on your hands as all rods have to be struck at once. Sandwiches are thrown down, oozing mayonnaise and salad over chocolate cup cakes, and by the time you have sorted it all out they have landed one fish and lost the other three.

Then comes the ceremony of photographing the poor creature who, now regretting his impulse to annoy a fishing widow, only wishes to get back into the water with all speed. The lucky angler who holds the fish for the camera puts his thumb into the carp's mouth.

'It gives them a bit of comfort, Mum. Something to suck on,' my son told me when asked why he used his thumbs in this way – and *before* he had eaten his sandwiches. It didn't look very comforted to me, quite the reverse in fact. Pity carp haven't got teeth, that's what I think.

Anglers rarely smile while they are having their photo taken for it's a very serious business. The exception being the youngest for this is the first carp he has ever caught. He grins in delight but he doesn't know the ropes yet and he will soon learn to look unsmiling and dignified.

There is the odd perk for a FW lakeside. When you get really fed up, after about ten hours and it starts getting a bit chilly, you can always pick blackberries in the appropriate season and hazelnuts if you can reach them. There is also the added bonus of silently betting which of the other anglers will be next to run half a mile round the lake, arriving breathless and frantic, to discover which flavour boilies your anglers are using so successfully. Just listen to the evasive answers your family churn out. It can be quite an education.

Carp Fever

Carp fever is not seasonal. It can last all year round for even in the close season there are books on technique to read and digest, boilie bases to make up and freeze, tackle to be refurbished and so on. The illness is very contagious and it takes only minutes to be infected. There is no known cure.

The symptoms are many and acute. If you are approached by an angler who greets you with 'Have a smell of this,' as he thrusts a home-made boilie under your nose, you should endeavour to remove your own anglers from the vicinity as quickly as possible for fear of contamination with the fever.

Victims will drive fifty miles in awful weather conditions, in order to check out a 'new' lake. Not to fish it at this juncture, but to assess the size and possible dietary preferences of the carp within it. They take careful note of the surrounding trees and shrubbery and mentally choose a swim that they will fish when they have had time to calculate the number and flavour of boilies required for a day's angling.

Another sign is a collection of flavourings in the

carpist's kitchen which have no culinary use. Labels with '1,000 × Concentrated' written on them are a dead giveaway. These plastic-bottled oils and jars of powder will be used, when the fever is at its height, to flavour and enhance each and every boilie.

A set of measuring spoons, a pipette and a squeezy bottle of liquid Hermesetas in case some of the carp are on a diet, are part of the vital equipment necessary for the flavouring session when boilies are carefully counted into small, plastic bags in readiness for the ceremony. Not the same number in each bag, there may be five in one, nine in another but the flavouring is added, accurate to the nearest drip, in a ratio to the number of boilies per bag. It can be like watching an artist at work, for the flavours are not only used separately, but intermixed to make a cocktail guaranteed to tempt the most elusive and discriminating carp.

It's all done with meticulous care, with many surreptitious glances from side to side – just in case there is a spy in the camp who will rush out and tell the world of the magic combinations. They roll the boilies about a bit within the bags and then inhale each one deeply, like a demented glue-sniffer. The ecstacy can be seen on their faces to such an extent that you may be tempted to use some boilie oil yourself, instead of the expensive perfume, which has been standing expectantly on a bathroom shelf for several years, waiting for a special occasion in the company of your angler.

I guarantee that you will catch your anglers gazing into the store cupboard, examining the tins of various pulses that you usually sling into stews when there is not quite enough meat to go round. If you are not vigilant they will slip a tin or two into a romper-suit pocket together with a tin of luncheon meat which *they* say is going to supplement their lunch, but you know they are going to throw in a lake.

Carp fishing during the winter months is an even more elaborate affair than the summer expeditions. The only advantage being that fishing widows are allowed to remain at home in the warm. They discourage us from going along, don't they? – probably because they don't want to put up with us wingeing about the cold all day – but the preparation is more demanding on our time and resources.

Thick soup or stew has to be prepared the day before in quantities so vast that it is impossible to procure enough vacuum flasks in which to store it. The acquisition of a cooker of some description is therefore vital so that your angler can reheat the soup as and when required. We know of an angler who bought a 'state of the art' portable gas cooker for his son's birthday present. The lad was hoping for a computer but hid his disappointment bravely and was allowed to go on several carping expeditions as a result.

When your angler has a source of heat, of course, he can pinch the only non-stick frying pan that you possess along with a couple of pounds of sausages, the bacon which should be used for family breakfasts during the week and a couple of dozen eggs. Teabags will be 'borrowed' – do you really want them back? – together with a couple of pints of milk and the only tin-opener in the house with which to open the tins of baked beans that may, or may not, be hurled on to the mounds of bread and butter already prepared and packed. You may, because of the deprivation of the tin-opener, develop an uncharacteristic craving for baked beans on toast yourself. It's just a psychological reaction. Try and fight it.

Two bivvies have to be erected at the lake, one for your angler and one for the boilies – and equipment –

so that everything remains dry and germ-free. This may mean that one tent has to be borrowed from a friend and you will be the one to do the borrowing because your angler will be at work. It's a good idea to phone round first. With a bit of luck you may find a friendly angler with flu who can't use his tent this weekend. He'll be less friendly if you tell him, when you return it, that your angler has caught a 25 pounder.

They'll take a sleeping bag – just in case the fishing is so good they decide to stay overnight – two Tilley lamps, one for heat and one for light, a couple of torches in case the lamp breaks down and then depart in the middle of the night, or so it seems, looking like Nanook of the North and loaded down with gear. They return, some twelve hours later, covered in mud, sweat and tears, freezing cold and hungry. How can they possibly be hungry? They took a week's groceries with them! They'll need unlimited sympathy and understanding as they relate their heart-rending tales of woe and disaster.

'Plenty of nibbles,' they will cry, plaintively. 'But they didn't appear to be feeding. We couldn't seem to hook anything.'

We know why, don't we? It's those boilies. Who wants to eat fruit for dinner in the depths of winter? The carp probably sucked a few and then spat them out again in disgust. Now if they had thrown in a nice steak and kidney pud . . .

Size Doesn't Matter

One autumn afternoon last season, while exchanging gossip with one of our lake bailiffs, I was privileged to witness the capture, from connection to landing, of a small but perfectly formed common.

Mick Brown was relating to me how he had fished the local ponds as a boy and, so engrossed was he in his narrative, almost misty-eyed with nostalgia, that it was a good few seconds before he realized that a gentle beeping was coming from the direction of one of his rods.

Suddenly, he snapped into action, instantly switching from raconteur to experienced carp angler. The half-told boyhood story was summarily dismissed and all powers of concentration centred upon the, by now, connected fish.

I watched, fascinated, as he played it away from the weed-beds, all the while offering soft words of encouragement and reassurance to his prey.

After ten minutes or so he knelt, almost reverently, at the water's edge to net it and revealed a truly beautiful nine pounder. The gold and silver scales seemed to reflect the autumnal hues from the surrounding, rapidly changing, foliage and with a slight mist forming in the late afternoon it was a magical moment.

Mick gently returned the carp to the lake, and within a matter of minutes had rebaited and cast out. He stood up, sighed deeply with satisfaction and returned his attention to me.

'Wasn't she a beauty?' he said. 'Now, where was I?' But the thread of his childhood fishing reminiscences had been broken by a small princess of a carp.

Size doesn't matter. Any man will tell you that.

Boilies for Beginners

Your junior carpists will get the urge to experiment with their baits and will develop an uncontrollable desire to make their own boilies – usually on a Sunday when the local tackle shop is closed for a well earned rest.

They will wait until you have dozed off after a hefty Sunday lunch and then proceed to decimate the larder. Flour, salt and water will be hurled into the Kenwood, together with a few drops of every flavouring in the spice cupboard – vanilla, lemon, almond, brandy, a soupçon of custard powder, a touch of gravy browning and a couple of spoonsful of peanut butter to aid the consistency.

They then try unsuccessfully to make small spheres with the ensuing glutinous mess. More than half of it will attach itself to their hair and clothing and it's not easy to shift, believe me, even with biological washing powder.

Eventually they will admit defeat, throw the surplus into the waste bin and demand that you telephone an angling friend who has been making his own boilies for years, and who has been known to bring tears of tedium to the eyes of fishing widows as he lectures on various flavourings – in the case of his own widow, the tears are brought about by some of the strange combinations and acrid aromas which regularly pervade her kitchen.

You will explain your problem briefly to this kindly natured man and before you can say 'artificial flavouring' he will be on the doorstep, armed with a polythene bag containing a pound or two of boilie-base mix, half a dozen eggs and a small bottle which contains all they will need as regards flavouring, enhancers etc. He won't tell you exactly what is in this bottle, however much you cross-question him, just that it is predominantly strawberry. He will explain that he was tempted to supply your youngsters with something which would cause you to call in the Health Inspector, but that he is too fond of you to put you through that particular trauma. He doesn't tell you that your whole house will smell of strawberries for the next several days.

Your expert will explain the aim, method and conclusion of the boilie-making art in graphic and lengthy detail until the junior eyes glaze over due to a surfeit of information – they can only concentrate for twenty minutes at a time – then drink a hasty cup of coffee with the Chief Angler while discussing the intended capture of the biggest and most elusive carp in the local lake and eventually head off home to his own boilie-making stint.

You will be forcibly removed from your own kitchen because the boys want to do it all themselves and you will only be allowed back in to clear up the mess when they have finished.

They use four saucepans at once, one for each ring on the stove, to speed up production and the fun begins in earnest. The mixture is stirred to the correct texture, chopping boards purloined to roll the boilies on and the first few are perfect if slightly unevenly shaped. The shape deteriorates as time goes by and they discover that the practical is not as easy as the theory. The last few are so enormous – the novelty will have worn off long ago – that you imagine they intend to stun the carp into submission with missiles rather than use the more conventional rod and line.

They will flop down exhausted after two hours in the kitchen but don't be tempted to tell them that is how you feel after cooking their Sunday roast – they will only gaze at you uncomprehendingly as you leave the comfort of your armchair and head for what used to be your kitchen.

It looks like a bomb site and the smell makes you gag but it only takes an hour to clear it all up and by now you should be anticipating the next stage in the game. It doesn't take long.

'If we go now,' they will plead, 'we can get a couple of hours' fishing in before the light goes – we can try out our boilies, we'll catch loads of carp. Please, please can we go? Now, if not sooner?'

It's the middle of winter, dark by four o'clock and it's now half past three. They will complain bitterly when you refuse permission, even allow the bottom lip to tremble slightly when you tell them to leave the boilies on a clean cloth, to dry out overnight, and then freeze them in the morning. They may throw a wobbler or sulk for ages, either way you are not in for a good time.

The week drags by. Every evening they will say 'only five more days to go,' 'four days and we can try out our boilies,' 'three days . . .' At last it is Saturday and they are up at the crack of dawn, well about seven-ish but it will feel earlier, and you will transport them, in freezing fog, to the lake. They will insist that you do not return until mid afternoon. They are hard. They are men. They have soup, hot chocolate and a mountain of sandwiches.

Go and get them about lunchtime – they will have had enough, I guarantee. The boilies have not tempted a single carp and even when you try to explain about the water temperature deterring the fish from feeding, they will not believe you and it must be that the flavouring wasn't quite right.

On the way home you will have to stop at the tackle shop so they can spend pocket money on more boilie-base mix – just in case they fancy making a few hundred more, but not today, they'll shove it in the shed where it will sit, for several months, waiting for inspiration to strike the juniors. It will become infested with weevils and if you look carefully you can see the mix moving about in the bag. Quite unnerving for an inexperienced fishing widow but do not be tempted to throw it away. Your juniors will tell you that the weevils would have added a certain piquancy to the bait and, since you were the one responsible for its disposal, it will be your fault if nothing is caught the next time they go for carp.

Boilie Cake

Some of the smells that fill the house after a boilie-making session can be pretty malodorous, particularly if they have used a fishmeal base and essence of squid or crab. The stench can linger for days at a time despite excessive use of air-fresheners and the leaving open of all doors and windows. It's not all bad news though, sometimes those flavourings can come in handy.

My boys went through several stages of bait experimentation and while they were trying to get it right used up all my cake flavourings – vanilla, almond, lemon, brandy, you name it they tried it.

I had already made up a basic madeira cake mix before delving into the bowels of my spice cupboard for the vanilla flavouring – only to discover that the boys had used every last drip of everything and replaced the empty bottles into the cupboard so that I wouldn't discover their crime until one of the rare occasions when I baked a cake.

In desperation, for they won't eat it neat, even plain old madeira has to contain vanilla, I went to the bait-making cupboard. Some of the more recent aromas had smelt quite appetizing.

I found a dozen or so little bottles with Kevin Nash's name all over them but I didn't let that put me off. I've spoken to Nashy several times on the phone and he seems a decent bloke. He wouldn't manufacture any-thing unfit for consumption, human or piscatorial, and besides, you only have to witness the loving care bestowed during the boilie-making procedure to understand the obvious devotion to quality of anyone involved in supplying bait.

The flavourings are extremely potent, 1,000–1 concentrate, just removing the lid from a bottle fills the room with an overpowering smell of the contents so a few drips should be enough to flavour a cake. Mega Tutti-Frutti seemed a good bet and I knocked up some icing flavoured with Big Strawberry.

You should try this cake. It turned out to be one of my better efforts and was eaten within a couple of days instead of ending up in a trifle.

Here's how to do it:

Ingredients: 8 oz self-raising flour
pinch of salt
4 oz unsalted butter
4 oz castor sugar
enough milk to make it gooey

Method: Cream butter and sugar, beat the eggs and add, a little at a time, to the bowl. Fold in the flour and salt. Throw in a little milk to which you have added half a teaspoon of Mega Tutti-Frutti. Fling the whole lot into a cake tin and bake for 1 hour 15 minutes.

The icing is a doddle but care is needed with the cochineal bottle. I made a birthday cake, years ago, which looked like a road accident, even the kids wouldn't eat it and at five years old they'll eat anything made of sugar. So, 8 oz icing sugar mixed with a tablespoon of warm water, a couple of drips of red food colouring and another drip or two of Big Strawberry does the job.

Try it. It's delicious.

Faith, Hope and Charity

'And now abideth Faith, Hope, Charity, these three; but the greatest of these is Charity.' An odd title, you may think, but take a minute to consider those three words for they epitomize the average carp angler's attitude towards his sport. My own anglers certainly qualify and, I suspect, so do a good percentage of carp anglers everywhere – especially during a long session. It is only faith, hope and charity which makes the whole business of carp angling such a pleasurable endurance test.

Faith, a strong belief that a carp will take the bait eventually, providing sufficient patience, expertise and perseverance are applied. Hope that the anticipated carp will develop a taste for the flavour of the month and turn out to be at least a twenty pounder. And charity, occasionally asked of other anglers, as and when required, and usually freely given. Not just the practical help that everyone needs now and again; a lift to the lake, cups of tea when fingers are stiff with cold and the stove won't light, the loan of a torch when batteries expire unexpectedly in the middle of a long, hard night, a fellow angler prepared to leave his swim for ten minutes in order to net the captive in an awkward place or to take the inevitable photograph, and so on – but the kind of charity that enables a rival, when he has caught nothing at all, to congratulate a more successful angler – and mean it!

My youngest, without a doubt, relied on these three daughters of the gods for an interminable, carpless fourteen weeks which began at the start of this season. Such was his faith that he refused to give up despite merciless mickey taking, from his brother and assorted friends, when he blanked time after time.

'Off to the lake again, Simon?' they would ask, patronizingly. 'Isn't it about time you caught a carp? There are loads in there. Why, only last weekend I had four thirteen pounders out – you must be doing something wrong. Try putting a boilie on the hook this time!'

The youngest pretended to shrug off all the ridicule and derisive remarks and carried on with his vigil. Every evening, after college until well after dark, together with night sessions every weekend, would see him at the lake trying unsuccessfully to tempt his prey – with just an occasional afternoon deviation towards pike fishing as light relief, but only if he was alone on the lake and unlikely to interfere with other anglers – with his carp rod out in a separate swim, just in case.

Big brother, in between good-natured teasing, offered sound but largely ignored advice – he's a very successful carp angler having learned quickly from experiment, his early mistakes and by gleaning hints from his peers. He gave freely of his own secret, infallible rigs and baits plus the loan of a primus stove as the nights became chilly and the summer diet of bottles of lemonade and sandwiches were spurned in favour of hot tea and tinned beans.

So, there he sat, the youngest, night after night. A lone sentinel guarding his swim with a jealous but meticulous eye. Taciturn when questioned, ungrateful for company unless it was short-lived and accompanied by food, while showing a determination which bordered upon bloody-mindedness – I can't think where he gets that from.

Towards the end of his long season of hope, there came a night of clear skies, cold air but with no wind to speak of and a full moon. Cousin Paul had insisted on going along to this particular session and was grudgingly allowed into the bivvie after he had paid his entrance fee with a couple of tins of Jumbo hot-dogs, several sachets of hot chocolate and a pack of playing cards with which they could while away the wakeful hours.

Myself, as a dutiful mother armed with a couple of fragrant parcels containing fish and chips, and Himself carrying only a fellow carp angler's avid curiosity, paid the boys a visit around suppertime. They were playing Newmarket, using items of tackle for side bets although there was no danger of loss for at the end of the game all the hooks, floats and weights are sorted out and returned to their rightful owners. We stayed with them while they fell upon the food as if they had not eaten for a week and listened as they regaled us with stories of monster carp who lived in the depths of obscure and remote British lakes – Paul had also brought along a book of 'fishy' tales – and, less spectacularly but with equal enthusiasm, about an adjacent angler's landing of a sixteen-pound common.

We were told that it was fortunate, in a way, that they hadn't caught anything yet – neither of them had remembered to bring a camera and no one would believe the capture of a fine carp, bearing in mind the youngest's track record so far, without photographic evidence. They would suspect family loyalty with his cousin as a witness, so it was just as well that they hadn't had so much as a knock.

By the time we were ready to depart homewards for our own evening meal, a friend from college had turned up to join our intrepid pair – bearing a coveted camera and begging admittance to the bivvie on the strength of allowing its use, if and when. It was unanimously agreed that they would be ready and waiting for me in the car park at noon on the following day so that I wouldn't have to climb two stiles and trudge across a cow-pat minefield to wake them up as usual.

To my surprise they kept their promise and were packed up and sitting like a row of large, green crows on the car-park fence when I arrived. 'Simon caught a twenty-one pound ten-ounce mirror,' they yelled as soon as I pulled up. 'Brilliant, isn't it?'

No one else had caught anything but they were unconcerned about that. They were overjoyed with a result for their erstwhile carpless companion and I had to endure a verbal action replay all the way home – which made little sense until later, when I managed to persuade them to speak one at a time.

They had, they said, been playing gin-rummy for matchsticks at 10.20 pm when the bite-alarm proclaimed the presence of a carp. A bitter struggle ensued, taking about twenty minutes from connection with the carp to landing it. Trevor had risked life and limb by climbing up and down a slippery, mud-covered bank while removing spare rods from the water; Paul had risked double pneumonia entering the lake up to his waist to meet the fish and net it, while Simon reigned, King of the Castle, victorious, dry and free from discomfort on the bank.

That, my friends, is charity in its purest form. Now they are all faithfully hoping that the bigger carp will be charitable enough to allow themselves to be caught.

Carp Before Marriage

A word of warning to new or prospective fishing widows. There is one aspect of marriage to a carp angler that no one bothers to tell you about and by the time you find out, you will have signed the register and it's too late.

Recently, I was told by an indignant and perturbed young woman that she had been cruelly abandoned towards the end of a candlelit dinner for two, just as she was contemplating slipping into something more comfortable, in favour of a seemingly imperative visit to a carp lake some fifteen miles away. Her man had received one of those telephone calls. Experienced widows will know the ones I mean.

She seemed bewildered and amazed that this could have happened to her, since she has only been wed for three weeks, and took the incident as a personal affront to her attractiveness.

I told her this is a fairly normal occurrence in carp-angling households. She should not condemn her mate, because these things are beyond his control and therefore not his fault. She should try to accept the fact that it's odds on she will always be compared unfavourably to a carp over thirty pounds – particularly if she doesn't struggle hard enough.

The poor girl has to become accustomed to these situations if the marriage is to be a harmonious one, for if you are partner to a carp angler there's always a chance that there will be a telephone call from a jubilant but frantic fellow enthusiast with a mobile phone who has just caught a monster and has forgotten to pack his camera.

I told her she was lucky that she was still at table and had not yet reached simmering point in the bedroom. Her lover could have leapt out of bed, pulled on a pair of jogging bottoms, hurtled down the stairs, jumped into the car and screeched off down the road to record on film a wondrous event for posterity leaving his fishing widow seething with a number of emotions, the predominant one being the desire to inflict serious injury.

She should be thankful for small mercies.

Origin of
Species

Deep in the Heart of Texas, USA, carp are looked upon as 'trash' fish. It seems incredible but I was told so, on very good authority, by some visiting friends who live in Bandera County, east of San Antonio. In fact, they said, there is a rule on their statute book categorically stating that if a carp *is* caught it must be destroyed – and they are always caught by accident, no red-blooded Texan boy would be seen dead fishing for carp.

When I asked them how this could possibly be, when in Britain carp are revered to an almost unhealthy degree, they told me that, in the area where they live, anglers prefer to hunt for catfish and because the carp monopolize the food supply, the catfish suffer as a consequence – hence the officially enforced destruction of as many carp as possible. My anglers were aghast and near to tears at this point.

Culls are occasionally organized before the carp-breeding season begins, so our American friend told me, because the waters in some parts of the USA, particularly the South, are considerably warmer than they are here so the carp reproduce at an alarming rate to the detriment of other fish. Killing them off is not the most popular job, apparently it is considered to be a chore, but someone has to do it and it's carried out with ruthless efficiency.

Since we know it is the temperature of the water that triggers off the reproductive urges of the carp, I asked my informants how the exterminators could tell when the breeding season was imminent. Surely, if the waters were *that* warm the fish would be at it all the time. There didn't seem to be a definite answer to that one, just a vague description of observing the first signs of spawning activity and then performing the dreadful deed before the rest of the carp got the urge and followed suit.

Texans love the sport that catfish provide, despite the fact that their carp, if allowed to survive, can grow to over fifty pounds – at least that's what they told me, but it may well be one of their Texan Tales. I imagine, at that size, it would be like trying to land a nuclear submarine – more sport than a jumpin' catfish, surely? Or maybe not, I'm no expert.

Our American friends were puzzled in the extreme when they were called upon to admire the multitude of photographs showing mid-twenty-pound carp. Even more amazed when they discovered that they were expected to exclaim deliriously over the paintings of carp species, churned out by my spouse during rare but inspired moments away from the lake. They smiled but shook their heads when shown the photo enlargements, proudly framed and exhibited, of a couple of thirty pounders clutched euphorically to the bosom of their captors, which grace our dining-room wall.

They showed the barest minimum of polite interest when told tales of stalking and preparing a bait, of the suppressed excitement while casting under a discriminate carp's nose and the thrill of its eventual capture.

I caught them exchanging quizzical glances with each other when they thought no one was looking and they were downright incredulous when informed of magazines entirely devoted to carp, requesting copies to take home to show their friends, their suspicions that the English are mostly one sandwich short of a picnic by this time fully augmented. 'The guys who thought that one up must be plumb crazy,' they said, gazing dumbfounded at Carp Society brochures. And the fact that certain of our private lakes are reserved exclusively for carp fishing, coupled with the fact that these venues cost an arm, leg and portions of lower torso to join, had them falling about.

We were loath to show them the paraphernalia required to make boilies in case their mouths dropped open any further, and as for bite-alarms etc – we didn't dare.

Instead, we began a discussion, fortified by several bottles of wine, about how the carp were introduced to 'foreign climes' in the first place.

Originally from China, we agreed, where the natives farmed them for food two thousand or more years ago, the carp spread across into Europe and eventually the monks brought them over to our shores from the Continent to stock them in stew-ponds where they bred, multiplied prolifically and thus provided sustenance for many.

From these 'wild' carp, which, my Texan chums insisted were the cause of all their piscatorial problems, other strains were developed, varying from the diverse mirrors, chunky little crucians and vigorous commons, through to the modern Japanese Koi. These oriental beauties are rarely used for sport fishing because they are a valuable commodity and are open to theft and subsequently yielding a hefty profit for the appropriator. They are kept, as a general rule, solely for their attractiveness and variety. Texas couldn't understand that either.

I mentioned our relationship with a local Chinese takeaway proprietor, who always asks about recent captures of carp whenever we venture into his establishment. He is only interested in the culinary side of things and almost slavers over the photographs produced upon request. Our American friends giggled at the idea of carrying around carp photos in a breast pocket, before blanching visibly at the very thought of eating a carp – they think of them as vermin and as far as they are concerned, it would be akin to consuming a rat. The Chinese, I told them, look upon baked carp as a delicacy, as do Jews and some Europeans. They changed the subject.

Eventually we all decided that it had been a mistake to introduce carp into the United States during the early nineteenth century, agreeing to differ on our reasons for arriving at that conclusion. From our point of view it seems such a terrible waste – my anglers speculated on ways of importing some of the hardier species to live in our own lakes. The American sentiments, of course, were more along the lines that carp should never have been allowed into the States in the first place.

It seems ironic that these beautiful creatures are so carelessly dismissed on the other side of the Atlantic while in Britain they are sought after, nurtured and respected.

Carp are a nuisance fish in America. Ain't that a shame?

Song of
the Carp

I'm playing leapfrog with my Chum,
When all at once – no kiddin', Mum,
These boilies suddenly appeared,
I'm tellin' you, it's really weird.
All day they landed in our swim,
Now, call us dense – a little dim,
But we don't understand the man,
He's got so many in his van.

He fires 'em our way with a catty,
Chum and me, we think he's batty,
Hundreds of the blessed things,
Hurts our tails and scrapes our fins.
All different flavours too, they are,
Some come near and some go far,
We ate as many as we could –
Some of them were rather good.

Well, me and Chum, we sat and thought,
He won't be happy till we're caught,
We'll just get hooked and then, that way,

He'll bugger off – leave us to play.
So we got caught a time or two,
It didn't hurt – it's what carp do,
But he kept throwing boilies in,
And then ate beans out of a tin.

We thought he's bound to pack up soon,
T'was nearly time for Harvest Moon,
But no, he only lights a lamp
And then begins to set up camp.
Well, we gave up soon after that,
But he came down to have a chat.
Talks quite a lot to us, you know,
P'raps he's nowhere else to go.

He sat there fishing through the night
We knew he wouldn't get a bite,
But, me and Chum we had a plan,
We'd try and please this angling man.
As the dawn broke, mist and rain,
We let ourselves get caught again,
He seemed so chuffed, could hardly speak,
He'll bring his mates as well, next week.

Some Lake
It Hot

It is the hottest day of the century – and where is the average fishing widow? Is she relaxing at home with a glass of iced tea and a punkah wallah doing the business? Of course she isn't. She is stuck in the middle of three miles of solid traffic with a full complement of frustrated carp anglers aboard.

'How long before we get there, Mum?' the youngest implores for the hundredth time from the back seat, after being told, an hour ago, to stop asking if we are there yet.

'Can't you take the back road?' sighs the Chief Angler, as if it is *my* fault that the world and his mother have decided to set out at the same time and in the same direction as us. We *are* on the back road – on the main road there's a *seven* mile tail-back, according to the travel report courtesy of local radio – let's count our blessings.

'I could easily cut you a sun-roof in this car, it wouldn't take five minutes with a hacksaw,' number one son tried to cheer me up but with complete disregard of our fickle British climate – I wouldn't like to try asking him to replace the cut-out bit if it rains.

After an hour, when we had travelled five miles, and ten to go, we at last emerged from the bottleneck – there's never any sign of what caused it, is there? – and proceeded at an exhilarating thirty miles an hour towards our destination.

As soon as the car started to move they began to discuss tactics, prematurely choosing swims for themselves – which was purely academic because we had no way of knowing how many other anglers were going to be there before us, particularly if they had travelled from the opposite direction without the inconvenience of traffic hold-ups. The discussions continued after we had arrived and were tottering around the mile perimeter of the lake-of-the-day, looking for somewhere to settle.

So much fishing time had been wasted during the journey that I was left to pitch camp single handed. They had more pressing jobs to do – tackling up and baiting the swims, walking round the lake trying to ascertain what the other anglers were using and if it was successsful. Just as I had finished making a cool nest for myself, they returned from the water's edge and flopped down in it, demanding cold drinks and crisp salad with their sandwiches. They'd got a hope!

You probably already know that it is never wise to assume that the chocolate biscuits will be safe, along with carefully wrapped egg sandwiches, nestling companionably in the cool box with a few sausage rolls. As soon as my back was turned and before we had left the house, my painstakingly prepared picnic had been hastily and unceremoniously decanted into a plastic carrier bag, to make way for the far more important boilie collection – and possibly maggots, sweetcorn and the occasional elderberry because the youngest hasn't yet acquired the necessary patience for carp fishing only, he's after roach too. No one mentioned their devious act and by the time I found out it was too late to salvage the food and too hot to argue.

I deemed it best to eat as much food as possible, as soon as possible, and for the rest of the day keep stomachs satisfied with cold drinks, which had been placed in a keep-net in the lake, augmented by anticipating thoughts of the sumptuous meal to be enjoyed when we eventually arrived home again – if I could summon up the energy to prepare and cook it, that is. The reason for this early banquet was a good one. The sandwiches deteriorated fairly swiftly, despite being shifted hourly into the shady bits as the sun moved round the brolly, and whose idea was it to bring along chocolate biscuits anyway? Mine?

The boilies (*et al*) remained in the cool box – cool, calm and full of flavour all day while our food decomposed slowly in the sun and it was almost with relief that I welcomed a couple of my son's very hungry friends at about lunchtime-ish, despite knowing how three young men can decimate a large picnic within mintues – at least the food wouldn't be wasted.

Once everything edible, rancid or not, had been consumed, the friends waved a cheery goodbye and departed for pastures new, or more likely the nearest pub and left me in peace. Except for a visiting dog.

The dog waited until I had very nearly dozed off in the quiet, sun-filled afternoon, then he jumped on me, frightened me out of my wits and demanded that I 'play'. His owner seemed to have become invisible. There was no hope of rescue and the dog was very persistent as he ran in and out of the lake in an attempt to get me to join in.

My anglers ignored my plight. The Chief Angler was

playing a big one, the juniors were softly calling encouragement without moving from the water's edge and the dog was throwing himself in and out of the shallows of a bit of the lake that, fortunately, no one wanted to use for anything else. The owner turned up after half an hour of this and apologized for his pet. I smiled weakly and told him, falsely, that there was no problem and that I had quite enjoyed the shower of cooling lake water received every time Fido demanded my attention.

Master slipped a lead on his hound and wandered casually towards my anglers with a verbal questionnaire about the day's action. They were not too happy to have an excitable dog prancing about near their precious tackle but answered politely enough, if somewhat tersely so that, after a few minutes, One man and His Dog got the message and departed.

Bloody dogs!' exclaimed my Chief Angler, indignantly. 'Fancy taking the dog for a walk to a carp lake. The bloke must have no sense at all!'

I was a bit miffed that he hadn't taken any notice of

the dog until it was within three feet of his fishing gear, but bit my tongue and, instead of a suitable retort, asked gently if it wasn't nearly time to head for home since the canine visitor had obviously broken some kind of spell.

Within half an hour we were negotiating our way out of the car park while I heaped blessings upon the head of a four-legged saviour. We hadn't timed it right this time either. The traffic was as heavy as ever – everyone else on the planet had decided to 'leave it until later to miss the rush'.

My anglers didn't notice the delay, homeward bound. They never do.

PART THREE

The Coarse Widow

A Day at the River – Feels Like a Decade

All kinds of coarse angling is enjoyed on river banks. Lakes are all very well, I've been told, for carp and tench but for pike, barbel, roach, rudd and perch you can't beat a stretch of river water. The sounds made by a flowing curent or a weir pool seem to give the anglers inspiration and it is possible to walk for miles to look for an infrequently fished spot.

Fishing widows should face these adventures with fortitude and go prepared for anything. The first priority is your own comfort and although this means toting a garden chair for several hundred yards along with armfuls of food and drink, it is well worth the struggle. No matter how thick a blanket, after a couple of hours spent sitting quietly and still – you are not allowed to make any sudden movements for fear of spooking the fish – the ground becomes harder and harder until every bone in your body aches.

You can't take everything that you may need, you'd never carry it, but a small first-aid kit is a good idea. In fact, it is wise to provide a kit for your anglers, whether you are with them or not, particularly if youngsters are involved in a fishing expedition. The menfolk won't think of it. Most anglers are too preoccupied with thoughts of bait supply and assorted rigs to anticipate minor accidents, so it is our responsibility to ensure, at least during the long sessions, that a small box is carried along with the rest of the tackle. It doesn't take up much room and should contain the following items:

Sun block: it's surprisingly easy to suffer sunburn when the fish are biting and they are sitting, enthralled, at the water's edge.

Eye drops: to ease sore eyes brought about by either staring at a float for too long or attempting to gaze through sun-reflected water because they have forgotten to take along the Polaroids.

Plasters: to soothe hook lacerations, bait needle punctures or an occasional disgruntled pike attack.

Antiseptic cream: for nettle strings in the absence of dock leaves, or insect bites. Also handy for application to grazed knees when the youngest slides, inadvertently and still kneeling, down a river bank while keeping hold of his rod.

A wet flannel: in a plastic bag, with which to mop up the youngest when, through boredom, he has eaten his weekend supply of chocolate bars in half an hour.

Paracetamol: for yourself if you go with them on a river trip. The headache starts during the tactics discussions in the car en route and increases in severity on arrival when your anglers hurl *sotto voce* curses in the general direction of boat owners, canoeists and/or swimming children who are, quite reasonably, taking advantage of the only water for miles around on a boiling hot day. They will, in fact, mutter abuse at anything that moves anywhere near the water that doesn't have gills. Take a large packet – you can safely repeat the dosage every few hours.

Your anglers will complain that you are making an unnecessary fuss, when you offer them a miniature medicine chest, and insist that they won't need any of it but there are always a few items missing after each fishing trip and if you are not there to keep an eye on things at least you will have peace of mind while they're away.

One word of warning, though. For goodness sake tell them that it's there. It's no good trying to insinuate a first-aid kit into a rucksack without informing the owner. We know of one young man who borrowed his father's fishing gear for a long session in bleak midwinter and spent an uncomfortable, I'd go so far as to say miserable, and unproductive twelve hours hunched inside a bivvy without a hot drink to comfort his shivering bones. He found out afterwards that buried in the bowels of his father's huge rucksack, two feet away, there was a fully primed Colman stove, a kettle, an enamel mug, tea bags, dried milk and sugar – even a small hot water bottle, but he hadn't bothered to look.

If you take a book to read it should be of the kind that does not require any degree of deep concentration. It would be no use trying to digest *War and Peace* on the river bank for you will be called upon to perform all manner of tasks and end up reading the same sentences several times. You must learn to turn the pages of your chosen novel very quietly or endure the wrath of the Chief Angler – you must understand that it is always and without exception your fault if nothing is caught or if a fish escapes.

Suitable clothing for a day at the river is important. Even consulting the weather forecast prior to leaving is no guarantee of success. You may yet be caught out – the meteorologists seldom get it right.

On one particularly gruelling day when I had foolishly

worn a sweatshirt and jeans, because it was cool and raining when we left home, the weather became gradually warmer as the day wore on, culminating in eighty degrees of bright and humid conditions by lunchtime, and I swore that never again would I be so stupid. My anglers refused to pack up and come home just because I was in danger of severe heat stroke. 'Take something off,' they said. Removing my wristwatch didn't help very much.

Now, I always dress in layers that can be peeled off or added to as the weather dictates. Even so, it pays to consider carefully. Do not wear colourful clothes, for example, or you will be banished to the outer regions of the fishing area for fear of startling the fish with your scarlet T-shirt – and they will complain that they have to walk a few yards every time they need a chicken leg. Best to stick to the colours of nature, ie, browns, greens, greys or black, that way no one can justifiably tell you to go away.

You may need to take spare pairs of knickers and jeans for yourself and almost certainly for the youngest for the simple reason that if anything important falls in the water – particularly the youngest – you will be the one to retrieve it if you have any sense.

If you don't offer to take an early bath your man will strip to his underpants and jump in the water to grope in the deep for precious items of tackle. Besides the week off work because part of his equipment has caught a chill, the sight of him thrashing about, near naked, in their habitat would frighten away every fish for miles and the certain rancour of the other anglers, by whom you appear to be surrounded, will make itself felt for several hours after the event. Far better to perform the operation yourself, gracefully and with the minimum of fuss.

Incidentally, they don't tell you until you are trying to clamber out, that the pike in that particular stretch of the river are the most voracious in the world, and have been known to take a man's – or a woman's – leg off with one bite.

The reason for the spare clothes is because if you are standing thigh deep waiting for your anglers to direct you towards the spot where the treasure fell in – your surroundings will look totally different from the water looking out, as opposed to the bank looking in – you will be concentrating on following their instructions and may, unthinkingly, bend over to feel around. You won't realize, until it's too late, that as your arms are not four feet long, the top half of your clothed body will end up under the water. Tucking the skirt of a sun dress into your knickers is not enough, you must be prepared to get thoroughly soaked and then change in the bivvy. Beats having to watch a pair of waterlogged underpants emerging, believe me.

Food, for a summer day out at the river, needs a fair bit of forethought and preparation, otherwise you may be told not to worry about it – 'We can do it the easy way.' The easy way, as far as my anglers are concerned is to hurl a couple of loaves into a bag, topped with bundles of sausages, bacon, burgers and tinned beans. All to be cooked – by guess who – on arrival at the venue. I know a gourmet angler who actually takes filleted breasts of duck, marinated overnight in orange or morello sauce together with parboiled potatoes and broccoli, all to be sautéed gently over the Colman.

For we lesser mortals, however, it makes far more sense to prepare all the food beforehand although there will not be a great deal of it consumed *in situ*, even if you are parent to a couple of young locusts, as I am. Most of it will be eaten in the car on the way home when you will be unable to hear the knocking of the engine over the noises of urgent munching, interspersed by 'if we had done this or that' and 'next time we'll try so and so', as you negotiate your ailing vehicle carefully around the corners in an effort to prevent them from choking to death as they chatter on and eat at the same time.

A large blanket might come in handy. To sit on, dispense food from or to wrap the youngest in when he/she invariably falls in the water and, if you don't have a bivvy, make sure that you take charge of the umbrella. It will rain at least once however short a time you stay – they will all fight over it and possession is nine-tenths of the law.

The comestibles should consist of single items, all individually wrapped, eg, hard-boiled eggs, filled rolls, chicken legs, small cakes, biscuits and so on. This is because the food must be held in one hand while the other holds or hovers over a rod– they rarely stop fishing just to eat – and crisps are tricky, not easy to manage unless they have both hands free. It has been known for the fishing widow to hold a sandwich to the angling mouth while both angling hands were occupied in playing a small bream – but only once.

A couple of dozen cartons of fruit juice and/or cans of lager are handy for emergencies. Consideration for their prey is the anglers' priority. It's put before everything else so they will leave their own needs until the last minute – they won't have the patience to wait for the kettle to boil when they are thirsty.

It's worth all the aggravation, for when you are stetched out, in dreaming mode, at the water's edge, the last thing you want to do is play about with food. You can just hand them a parcel of something and they'll go away and leave you alone.

If you think that the suggested amount of equipment for a day out seems a bit extreme, let me tell you that a few hours on a river bank seems like a decade and it will be your fault if something needed is not available. The whole issue seems such a waste of time, for at the end of the day the keep-net is hoisted up while the fish are counted and scrutinized before these unfortunate creatures, having been imprisoned away from their families for the day, are released into the river. Confused and with no sense of direction or humour, they wander gratefully away only to go through exactly the same experience next weekend.

Cereal Killers

Keep an eye on your Cornflakes at all times – and Shredded Wheat, Krispies, Puffs, Bix – in fact any cereal that you happen to have in the house. Turn your back for five minutes and it will all become an unrecognizable, anonymous heap of crumbs to which water will eventually be added in order to produce soggy handsful of ground-bait.

My own breakfasts are guaranteed safe, at the moment, for a limited period because of a husband in the advertising game. It won't last but, at least, I'll be able to rest easy in my bed for a few weeks. We rarely get free samples of any advertised commodities, which is a shame because hubby has been known to deal with high-powered cars, state of the art domestic appliances and expensive watches, but he received an unexpected bonus recently which perked him up no end.

A few months ago the agency had executed a campaign for a cereal company and, as a consequence, a couple of dozen boxes of various cereals had been delivered for a photographic shoot. The innards were removed and discarded, unopened, while the box fronts were used for the business end.

I received a phone call, one afternoon, from Himself who asked me how much a packet of cereal costs. Derek is not a 'new man', thank goodness – he's never set foot in a supermarket in his life, too busy fishing, and so hasn't a clue how much money I spend on food each week. He gulped a bit when I informed him that the average box of cornflakes was about £1.20ish – more if the cereal included nuts or fruit.

He didn't tell me why he wanted to know, but I'm used to strange questions being asked – I've got to the stage where I just answer and forget about it.

Turned out that he had discovered a heap of cereal-box contents in a corner of the studio and was deliberating on whether or not it was worth the effort of carting them all home. He decided that it most certainly was, given the exorbitant price of grain. He asked if anyone else wanted them and on receiving a negative – no pun intended – proceeded to empty them into a photographic bag, merrily scrunching so as to fit it all in. His colleagues threw him pitying glances from time to time – no doubt thinking we are really hard up – until he told them what he intended to do with the resulting mess.

His bounty was brought home, fifty miles on the train, and he spent an hour in the kitchen putting it all through the food processor – well, most of it, quite a bit ended up on the floor. Like I said, he's not domesticated in the slightest degree and I've never bothered to try to house-train, I quite like him as he is. So, it was the first time he had used the appliance and it took a bit of practice before he managed to work out which of the multitude of knobs produced the best result.

He filled up half my supply of freezer bags – ordinary polythene bags were not good enough, this

precious commodity (free!) had to be looked after –
no freezer burn allowed, the fish wouldn't like it –
and now a whole drawer of the freezer is taken up by
bags of cereal powder to be used eventually as
ground-bait.

'Think of the money you've saved!' he crowed and it
was a minute or two before I realized that, indirectly,
he was right. For a while he might leave the family's
cereal alone.

It seems as if every cupboard in the house contains
some item connected with fishing and it can only get
worse. Our local cash'n'carry warehouse has recently
opened its doors to lesser members of the public.
Anyone could join who was self-employed, their advert
in the local paper said – there was no need any more to
prove that one ran a bed and breakfast or a grocery
store. Any kind of business would qualify.

Seemed like a good idea to me, so I rang them up.
'Are you registered for VAT?' they asked me. 'Do you
have a business card?' The answer to these questions
was a definite 'no'. They hesitated, not keen to let a
lowly, freelance journalist through their hallowed por-
tals.

'I'll buy all my office equipment from you,' I pleaded.
'I write for several magazines and' – a moment of black-
mailing inspiration – 'the local newspaper, twice a
week, so if you don't let me join . . .'

They invited me to attend their office with proof. I
took my eldest, wearing a Southend Angling Centre T-
shirt, copies of *Carpworld* and *Improve Your Sea Angling*
together with a couple of cuttings from the paper.
There was no problem. They obviously knew a thing
or two that I hadn't even thought of but was soon to
find out.

Dave had been press-ganged into coming with me

because, although I had the cash, he was there to carry – about time he did something useful. So, after all the formalities of form filling, proof of identity, specimen signatures and so on, we were let loose into the warehouse where I was prepared to wander amiably around and just look until I saw something that I needed. Not so, number one son. He made a beeline for a nine-kilo bag of dog biscuits. We don't own a dog but Pedigree Chum mixers are often used as bait and have been on my grocery list for some time now so I was prepared for those.

The next stop was the cake flavouring department where he gazed in rapture at the array of spices, oils and colourings on offer. Various cereals, dried milk products, semolina, giant catering packs of pulses and equally enormous tins of pork luncheon meat were considered – not the ordinary stuff which is hurriedly, and if you're lucky, thrust between two slices of bread and offered to you for riverside lunch together with a cup of lukewarm tea. Nothing so economical. The fish must be tempted with the most expensive brand. You know the one – begins with S and ends in M.

All these items suddenly seemed to become a vital part of number one son's diet together with assorted crisps, biscuits and a variety of instant pot thingies to which, I realized later, he could just add hot water for an immediate lakeside banquet. Then there was the beer section . . .

We emerged into the vast car park having spent a large amount of my money – he's never got any spare cash – on a trolley load of stuff that I didn't want. They knew! The cash'n'carry people knew the probable outcome as soon as we mentioned angling. That's why they let us in.

On arrival at home we then had to find somewhere to

stash it all. Like I said, every single cupboard received a contribution and the house is awash with cereal in one form or another.

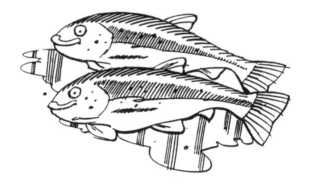

My Kingdom For a Bivvy

We enjoy summer fishing Sundays in comparative luxury these days. When I think back to the time when we would have to wait at a bus stop, for the first early morning vehicle out of town, clutching rods, tackle, umbrella, food and water, a pushchair and assorted strength nappies together with a toddler who had been rudely awakened from a disturbed night's sleep – David never slept for more than four hours at a time and was, as a consequence, permanently tetchy until a fishing rod was placed in his hot, little hand – it makes me wonder how I coped with it all.

A few years on, when our second son was about three we managed to get hold of an old Morris Marina which was rust infested but just about reliable enough to transport us as far as the nearest river – what more could we want? We still had nothing much in the way of comfort at the water's edge and I lost count of the number of vacuum flasks smashed, usually by me as I threw down the huge food bag with relief on arrival at their chosen spot. I accepted the fact that a day's fishing, which subsequently produced a maintained equanimity for all parties, was worth a few hours of discomfort.

The rods and reels were of the best quality, of course, but the brolly leaked and we only had one decent chair between us. You can guess who comandeered that so the rest of us had to sprawl on an old blanket which was spread adjacent to the most promising swim. Why is it, that no matter how carefully you study the ground before laying the blanket, there is always a huge rock, right in the middle and just where you decide to sit down?

A brolly-tent seemed a good idea in theory, so we borrowed one from a friend for one river excursion and it was wonderful. I curled up inside it with the latest Dick Francis and a hard-boiled egg and enjoyed twenty minutes of perfect peace until the youngest, who had been trying to hang upside down from the footbridge over the river, suddenly spotted the tent and wanted to play Cowboys and Indians, Spies, Turtles – anything that involved getting in and out of the tent and making very loud 'per POW' noises. Much to the annoyance of the Chief Angler, I needlessly add. Then it rained and we found that three long-legged people and a Spy do not fit into one average-sized brolly-tent.

That's when the CA decided that it might be a wise move if he went fishing on his own in future and my troubles began with trying to placate two small boys who had, seemingly overnight, had all their privileges removed. I had to learn, and pretty darned quickly, how to put maggots on hooks and to use a disgorger.

It took a number of years to achieve a reasonable car, a cool box, a Colman stove and couple of bivvies. Like I said, comparative luxury and well worth waiting for.

Beginners Please

The day will dawn when your youngest will be bitten by the angling bug. They go along on family fishing days out and show a mild interest but fanaticism will set in sooner or later – and it is only a matter of time. It happened to Simon, my youngest, a few years ago. Just when I thought that he was 'different' and going to be a comfort in my old age – it struck, if you'll pardon the pun – and I found myself going through the same rituals and ceremonies endured several years previously with his brother.

Cousin Paul, who was the same age and near enough at the same stage of angling development, spent so much time in our house discussing the theory of saving up and consequently purchasing a day ticket at a local lake 'one day in the holidays' that we thought he had moved in permanently.

After a few weeks they managed, between them, to glean sufficient equipment from various members of the angling circle. 'Anything you want to throw out, Dad?' 'I'll try to mend that broken reel.' 'If I untangle that, can I have it?'

They were desperate to try it all out, couldn't possibly wait another three weeks until the school holidays began, so I was soft enough to give up one of my precious Sundays in order to cart them the five miles to the lake – if only to put an end to the constant 'When can we go? Can we go tomorrow?'

The day before the planned expedition was spent in a state of high excitement and avid preparation. The youngest ran a bath. Not for himself – he'd had a lick and a promise – but purely to test the depth and angle of the floats on the already made-up rigs because it would save time when they arrived at the venue.

My suggestion that it might have been more environmentally friendly to fill up a bucket, test the rig in that and hurl the water over the flowerbeds was scornfully rejected as unrealistic. He actually cast into the bath – *you* try casting into a bucket!

The larder was raided as a matter of course, for they had seen their elders do this as an essential part of the preparation ritual. They removed the usual cans of sweetcorn and luncheon meat and then systematically gazed at every tin – just in case the contents might attract a small tench. I told them firmly that meat balls, sliced peaches and rice pudding are not ideal bait and that under no circumstances were they allowed to take them along 'just in case'.

Come the day, Paul arrived at the crack of dawn, rod in hand and raring to go. Simon had been ready since last night's bath time. We had to wait until the corner shop opened before we could go anywhere else – because the boys, pre-angling mode, had found it impossible to venture more than half a mile without a full complement of crisps and fizzy drinks. They hadn't yet experienced the 'while I'm fishing, I don't eat' syndrome.

One of them bought the *Sunday Sport* to read in the car on the way to the river. They giggled and stared at 'big chests' for a couple of miles and then returned to the scrutiny of tackle-box contents. When they arrived at their chosen spot the 'big chests' were discarded as the fish beckoned irresistibly.

The best swims were situated on the other side of the river and we tottered, with tackle precariously balanced, over an extremely narrow and muddy lock gate, a bit too close to the water for comfort – one slip and their precious equipment could be lost for ever in the deep, not to mention the risk to life and limb if they fell in. They were, however, extremely careful – they were carrying the bait.

At home, they are constantly hungry – no matter what the time of day or night, and I had catered for that, but riverside they were too engrossed to give food a passing thought. Eventually I had to order them to use their mouths for eating instead of discussion before one, or both, of them faded away, but even crisps and chocolate were passed over while the youngsters concentrated, instead, on giving the fish in the lake a decent lunch of sweetcorn, luncheon meat and maggots.

After a careful cast or two, small handsful of sweetcorn were confidently thrown into the swim. They had been told that this is a foolproof guarantee of success and waited expectantly for a result.

They waited for only a few minutes per cast and, after every one, wiped the residue of sweetcorn/maggot juice down clean jeans because they were too absorbed to trot the few yards, back to base, in order to retrieve a tattered towel brought expressly for the purpose of mopping up unspeakable things.

At the end of the day they were exhausted and almost complete silence accompanied our journey home

– worth all the hassle of a day out in anybody's book – they were content to have caught nothing at all, just being there was enough, at this stage, and within sight of home, began to discuss the next trip.

Several hours were spent in cleaning rods and re-organizing their tackle boxes, during which time they told me, several times over, what a fantastic member of the human race I was, making it blatantly obvious that I should succumb to their flattery and promise another fishing expedition almost immediately. We agreed that the next weekend seemed to be a good time. I couldn't help it – it's not often I receive so much praise and appreciation.

Join the Club

The answer to all the inconvenience of carting your youngsters here, there and everywhere is membership of a fishing club. It's a wonderful idea, not only to preserve your sanity but to give the juniors a bit of independence. No longer will you have to sit with them for hours on end, making admiring noises every time they catch anything – no matter how small.

There are usually a number of species inhabiting club waters so, if the kids don't have the patience for carp angling, they can dangle for other more co-operative fish. This means that you can transport them to the club lakes and leave them there, having first made sure that the venue is bailiffed, secure in the knowledge that they will be safe until you care to go and collect them – well, safe-ish – bearing in mind the proximity of a vast volume of water and an accident-prone nephew.

You should try and find a club that is reasonably local because there is no firm guarantee that you will just make the one trip per day – or two, if you count the one to pick them up. Let me give you an example.

Maggots had been bought the day before. They can

rarely afford a packet of baby boilies, sometimes used to tempt tench, and the Chief Angler has a habit of hiding his minuscule spheres of tutti-frutti inside the piano, safe from sticky fingers, so the juniors have to make do with whatever is available. They assumed that a supply of tinned sweetcorn still waited expectantly in the larder, not realizing that it had been used by the Chief Angler and his first mate at the weekend, so it was a matter of extreme urgency to visit the open-twenty-four-hours-a-day Asian grocer, in order to buy a tin for the junior Club Water visit.

It would have been wasting valuable fishing time to come home again, as the grocer's is on the way to the lake – so a tin-opener and a plastic bag were taken along at the outset. Tinned sweetcorn was carefully decanted, by the youngsters, into a plastic bag while I was travelling along the arterial road at sixty miles an hour – the empty tin and the opener being placed soggily into my handbag for disposal when I made it home again.

On arrival at the lake I had to give them a hand to shift the mountain of gear which appears to be necessary – dare I say vital – for eight hours or so of serious angling and, having seen them settled in, I staggered back to the sanctuary of the car to drive peacefully home for a few hours of welcome solitude, knowing that they would be happily obsessed with trying to tempt any aurally challenged fish in their vicinity. At this stage, they still found it difficult to lower their voices, on a permanent basis anyhow, despite being 'reminded' by other anglers.

Everything appeared to be hunky-dory – until I arrived home and noticed the yellow plastic bag staring accusingly at me from the back seat where it had been left in the excitement of the day. Was I idiot enough to drive all the way back to the lake with the coveted sweetcorn? Of course I was.

On my arrival, the youngest informed me that tragically he had dropped his brand new bait knife into the lake. I pointed out that he didn't need a knife for maggots and sweetcorn – particularly maggots – but he went on to reveal his innermost feelings. He loved that knife, it was his pride and joy. He begged me to bring his large magnet with me when I returned in the evening to collect him so he could dangle it in the vicinity of where the knife was dropped and hopefully recover it.

There are two hopes, we know that – Bob and No – but the magnet was dutifully delivered at the appointed time and patience summoned while he frantically dangled for ten minutes or so. No knife, but loads of drowned hooks attached to tangled line and 'deep joy' some of it was wound round a small float, so the exercise was not a complete waste of time – from his point of view at least.

After a few more visits they became a little more streetwise, or lake-wise might be a better phrase, and having previously gone through the trauma of running out of bait by midday they prudently equipped themselves with a gas burner, a container of water, a packet of boilie-base mix and several small phials of various flavourings, filched while the Chief Angler's back was turned. A production line was set up on the bank and attracted anglers from all corners of the lake since the boys had had a reasonably successful day. The juniors went into business. I was only thankful that they hadn't found a dead creature and attempted to breed their own maggots – but who knows what the future holds.

Inspired by the success of the lakeside boilie venture, my youngest – who has a talent with electronics – went into bite-alarm construction mode. A pair of 'grown-up' bite-alarms are expensive and he knew better than to even think about it, let alone ask. His only recourse was to make his own.

The prototype was a cumbersome affair which worked perfectly but used one of those large twelve volt batteries – it needed a tackle box of its own to live in – so plans were drawn up, pocket money advanced and the local electronics shop haunted for an hour until he had gathered together all the components necessary to manufacture a more compact model.

The finished bite-alarm looked, sounded and performed just as well as the expensive variety – it cost £6.50 to make and we didn't waste the prototype. It is in constant use as a front-door bell – appropriately enough in an angling household. It has the disadvantage of causing all angling arms to strike involuntarily every time we have a visitor, but you can't have everything and the youngest has sold quite a few bite-alarms to his friends. We're working on the market for door bells.

Membership to a club is worth all the aggravation, the constant drone of discussion about baits, rigs and tactics. It dispenses with the poring over maps for any small blue bits hitherto unexplored. You know where they are, roughly what they are doing and they are out in the fresh air. They learn patience, respect for wildlife, consideration for other anglers and eventually self-discipline – a hard enough lesson for any of us. More to the point, they are not underfoot all day, demanding money for videos to watch, cinema tickets and several hot meals through boredom.

Any kind of fishing is a great hobby for youngsters and eventually they grow up, go off on their own and leave you in peace. It's well worth the membership fee.

Gone Fishin'?

Joining a club is not all good news, mind. Not for your Chief Angler if the whole family belong to the same one. Desperate to be alone, they find themselves accompanied by their youngsters every time they set foot out of the house.

As I drove into the club car park one evening, prepared for taxi duty, I waved to an angling friend of ours who returned my greeting but not with his usual verve.

'Wassup, John?' I called out of the car window. 'Blanked again?'

'Blanked? I wouldn't mind if I'd blanked!' he cried. 'I haven't had a chance to get in the water yet and I've been here since two o'clock. It's them kids!'

Apparently, he had generously offered to take his two young sons off wifey's hands for twenty-four hours. Half an hour later his sons were practically on bended knees.

'Can my mate come too, Dad?' from the eldest. 'You said he could last week.'

'And mine,' piped up the youngest. 'I've told him how brilliant you are and he's asked his Mum and everything.'

What could the poor man do but agree to the additional mouths to feed. So, John is now responsible for four youngsters, who all want to fish different lakes in the complex, while the parents of the aliens are rubbing their hands together with glee, having successfully farmed their offspring out for the day – and night. No doubt they hastily arranged a second honeymoon or something equally sinister.

Meanwhile, back at the lake, John has single handedly erected three bivvies in two different venues, made a dozen bacon sandwiches only to be told after they had been eaten that the kids were still hungry and would die if they didn't get at least a bag of chips when the chippy – half a mile away – threw open its doors. He has disentangled lines from exploded reels, disgorged small roach, answered fairly good-naturedly when approached, every ten minutes, with 'Da-a-ad!' and has been generally rushed off his feet – a condition usually only conducive to fishing widows.

The next morning, he told me, his wife was going to impersonate the cavalry and collect the youngsters at about lunchtime-ish, leaving John to enjoy a few hours' peace and quiet.

'Trouble is,' he told me. 'By then, I won't be able to concentrate because she only collects the kids and I know that, sooner or later, I've got to dismantle the bivvies, clear up their swims, load all the gear into the van and sort it out when I get home. Then, when I want to go on my own, mid-week, she says "Oh, you're going fishing *again*, are you?" What does she mean, again?'

The following weekend, there he was once more. This time, he told me, he had thought that it might be all right. He had weaned his two young sons away from their mates and so anticipated a reasonably relaxed, pleasant day out carp fishing, even managing to get his own tackle wet – if you get my drift – after settling down his offspring.

An hour into the session and Eden, the eldest and eleven years old, decided to adjust his set-up. That was fine by John, while the boy was engrossed he was leaving his father alone. All was not well, however, for Eden had attached a fifteen-foot hook-length to his line so when he tried to cast out, rod over one shoulder, hefty throw forward, the hook remained where he had laid it on the ground behind him.

John took him aside and told him to shorten the hook-length a tad – like a couple of yards or three. Eden spurned all offers of help, preferring to perform the operation himself, meanwhile placing his rod against a convenient bush for safety.

When his father took another look to see how his son was faring, he couldn't believe his eyes. The rod had been leaned over a bramble with no inhibitions and several yards of surplus line, with the aid of gravity, had percolated down into the bowels of this huge and malevolent thorn bush.

'You 'kinidiot!' yelled John. 'There's no way we can get that out, not with the rig on. We'll have to cut it off and start again.'

'I'm fed up with fishing,' retorted Eden. 'I hate it so much, I'm never, ever going again. Erm, have you brought your match rod, Dad? I've left mine at home.'

After being attacked by the bramble and a good half an hour later, John had settled into his trusty bed-chair, heaved a sigh of relief over the fact that his son and heir was content at last – and glanced over to where the youngest was roach fishing three swims away.

Leon was sitting motionless, head down to his chest and a look of pure misery on his face. 'I knew what was up with him,' John told me. 'He'd tangled and was afraid to ask for help. Couldn't blame the poor kid after I'd cursed at his brother.'

He got up, resignedly, from his bed-chair and began to walk over to Leon's swim. The boy, on spotting his father's approach, promptly stood up and moved fairly swiftly to meet him.

'How's it going?' asked John, diplomatically.

'It's a bit slow, Dad,' replied Leon.

'You've tangled, haven't you? Never mind, I'll come and sort it out.'

'No! No! It's all right, honest. I can do it – it's only a little tangle.' Leon was panic-stricken in case he was next in line for a telling off.

John picked up rod and reel and examined the culprit.

'A bit slow, you say? That's not slow, boy. That's *dead*!' Somehow line had become entangled around every protuberance of the reel – even inside round the cogs. This was no ordinary bird's nest. This was a dismantling job for SuperDad when he had an hour or so to spare.

John told me this story with obvious great affection for his boys but it was at the start of the school summer holidays and he will have several more weeks of incident to cope with. It's a hard life, isn't it, girls? Still, with all this practice he'll soon be a better fishing widow than any of us.

Beware the Pike Angler

If you are really lucky there will come a day in the depths of winter – well, all right, more likely late November, but it can feel like winter – when you will be plucked from your cosy nest in front of a roaring log fire and wrested away from the anticipated bottle of wine and epic film on TV. As a special treat, you will be taken to the nearest river to go pike fishing.

'The fresh air will do you good,' they tell you as you struggle into moon boots and thermal everything. 'That north-east breeze is really invigorating.'

It's invigorating all right. The grass is still slightly cruchy underfoot, where the hazy sun has yet to penetrate the unforecast ground frost of the previous night. The wind is so strong that all the trees are pointing towards Mecca – although they say it will drop by lunchtime – and if the pike have got any sense at all they'll all be snuggled up somewhere with a good book. It's a good idea to take along a duvet or sleeping bag to wrap yourself in, several flasks of hot soup and at least one of whisky to keep out the cold.

Pike must be one of the most misunderstood fish in

the river. You can't help feeling sorry for them. They are hunted down with almost primeval ferocity and although they are not the most attractive of creatures, looking as if they need a good orthodontist and a nose job, they would probably be very good-natured if they didn't have to put up with aggravation received from manic anglers.

Pike-fishing expeditions are the ideal time for fishing widows to sit and meditate. There is nothing else to do. Reading is impossible for, even huddled inside the bivvy, there is a serious draught which will blow anything into the river and then you will be in deep trouble for frightening the fish. Your only recourse is to contemplate the meaning of life or at least ask yourself why on earth you are sitting there in the first place.

You will have to answer the call of nature at least once during the day – all that soup will take its toll. In the summer months it is uncomfortable, to say the least, but in the winter it is downright embarrassing. Everyone knows what you are up to by the cloud of steam that surrounds your chosen spot and you get remarks from strange men as you trudge back to your anglers.

'Better now, love?' they call out kindly – and we all know that they mean well but it certainly puts you off going again for the rest of the day.

When the pike do bite you have to admit that it's quite exciting to watch. They certainly put up a fight, poor little devils.

My anglers don't use live bait when I'm with them – seeing a dead smelt on the end of a hook is enough for me – they usually wait until I've gone for the customary 'after soup' three-mile hike to sneak on a small, wriggling roach.

It can take up to half an hour to land a decent-sized

pike and the anglers are almost as exhausted as the fish by the time they have made it surrender.

As soon as the pike is on the river bank they may use something called a 'pike-gag' – it looks like a large, open-ended safety-pin which they thrust into the pike's mouth in an effort to keep its mouth open while they use the 'Deep-Throat' disgorger. Enough to make anyone gag – it's no wonder that the pike harbours more than a little resentment towards its captors and fights so hard not to be caught.

The inevitable photography session is over within a few seconds because the pike is trying to get his own back and you may think that you can go home now – you might even catch the end of the film.

Forget it. They have heard a rumour that there is a twenty-five pounder lurking in the deep water. It's only a matter of time before someone catches it and they are determined to have a go, regardless of the fact that you are rapidly developing frostbite and have just run out of whisky.

Just as twilight falls and you are packing up to go home there will be a violent knocking on the one rod left out until the last minute 'just in case' and your anglers will begin the ritual war-dance up and down the river bank. It should be set to music, Michael Jackson's got nothing on them.

Eventually, after much effort and plenty of bad language the Chief Angler lands a very large disgruntled pike.

'I told you it was in there,' he says, smugly. 'Well worth waiting for, wasn't it?'

He may even forget himself sufficiently, such is his euphoria, to permit a half smile on the triumphantly taken photograph.

There will be an inquest on the way home in the car,

which carries on for several hours after you have cooked and served dinner, and plans made for the following Sunday because number one son now wants to catch the same fish as soon as possible – it appears to be a matter of life and death.

A hip-flask of whisky is not going to be enough next week, either – take the whole bottle.

Ducks 'n' Drakes

Hubby had a week off work recently so we spent a few days at our club water. Not quite true. He spent a few days – seven actually – at our club water and I went to sit with him for an hour or two on the last day. The weather was extremely hot so I did absolutely nothing, just sat and observed the wildlife and chatted to other anglers when they walked round to see how my Chief Angler was doing.

There is a family of ducks who live on one of the lakes, the one where we were camped, and I was told as soon as I arrived that one of the babies had fallen foul of the first cast-in of the day. 'They were all hungry,' my Chief Angler told me, 'and dived on the boilies as soon as I threw 'em in. Poor little mite got himself hooked and I had to net him and sort it out while his mother was having a go at me from the water – really gave me what for, she did.'

She obviously bore no grudge, though, for as I threw a couple of sandwich crusts in the water, she brought her four little 'uns over to see us. They all quackled at once – quack is what grown-up ducks do, the young ones quackle. Listen to them and you'll understand what I mean – so I fed them with bits of sandwich and as I had finished doing so Mick Brown, one of the bailiffs, strolled by for a chat.

'Where's the drake?' I asked him, 'All the ducks on the lake seem to be female.'

'I don't know,' Mick told me. 'There were three of them a couple of months ago. So keen to mate, they were, that they were chasing Daisy up and down the paths. One of them must have succeeded 'cos she laid sixteen eggs. 'Sfunny though. As soon as the eggs started to hatch, they buggered off!' Ring any bells, ladies?

'They've probably spent too much time observing anglers,' I said. 'Where are the other twelve ducklings, then?'

'Only eight hatched out,' said Mick. 'One went to a pike. Don't know what happened to the other three but I think the coots had something to do with it. Horrible family the Coots!'

He made it sound as if noisy neighbours had moved in next door. Poor bloke. Being a lake bailiff in hot weather is obviously getting to him.

Mounting Tench-ion

By a strange coincidence fishing for tench has, for our family, always been incident strewn. In fact, I have come to expect trouble and my stomach lurches with apprehension every time my anglers tell me that this will be a tench session.

The eldest, having inherited a gene from his father which enables him to sit very still for long periods of time, spends many hours – sometimes days – camped out at a water's edge. The fish are no respectors of human sleep patterns and, if the urge takes them, will feed at any hour of the day or night.

One summer weekend David had been settled in at the club lake for forty-eight hours, after carp mainly but he wasn't fussy, he told me, a decent tench would please him just as much. Due to a disturbed night he had retired to his sleeping bag around mid-morning in order to catch up on his rest and went out like a light.

Forty-five minutes later he was woken by a beeping bite-alarm and, still half asleep, ran bare-footed down the bank to strike the fish, stubbing his toe on rock, or so he thought.

The fish was netted and weighed – a tench weighing six pounds and he was so pleased that he didn't feel any pain in his left foot, probably because of the shot of adrenalin released by the body every time a fish is struck.

After checking the fish's mouth and its whole body he went to put it back in the water. It was immaculate but his brother, who had sensibly spent a comfortable night in his own bed and ventured lakewards after breakfast, insisted that it was bleeding quite heavily and that the unhooking mat was covered in blood. David knew that he had checked out the tench thoroughly and there had been no signs of blood at all so, while telling his younger brother not to be so stupid, he gently eased the fish back into the lake.

It wasn't until he went to get back into the bivvy that he noticed, while drying his feet off, that his left foot was covered in blood. We found out later that he had not stubbed his toe on a rock after all. It was a rusty, old sweetcorn can, half buried in the clay which had almost severed one of his toes. Luckily his feet were still numb from the cold dew on the grass so he felt no pain.

Meanwhile, I was at home and completely oblivious to all the drama occurring just a few miles away. Until the phone rang and on the other end of it panted my youngest. He had run half a mile uphill, to the nearest telephone box. He suffers with mild asthma in the summer months and the unaccustomed exercise had brought on an attack.

Wheezing and gasping he managed to convey that I was needed urgently at the lakes. He said something like 'Mum! Get down here quick! Dave's cut his toe off and he's got to go to hospital now!'

I have never driven so fast and arrived at the lake

some ten minutes later, having overtaken everything that happened to be in my path. I'm usually a patient driver but, by this time, I was worried sick about the amputee, my fears augmented by the knowledge of what could happen if I didn't get to the youngest at the start of an asthma attack.

Fortunately, cousin Paul, who had studied first aid while doing a stint with the Army Cadets, had calmly taken over in my absence, bandaged the injured foot in his T-shirt – the only clean bit of cloth that they had – and calmed down the asthma victim after making sure he had used his inhaler correctly.

By the time I arrived, breathless and frantic, everything was under control but before we could proceed, at a more reasonable pace, to the Casualty unit I had to listen to a graphic capture, so wasting precious minutes. The doctor on duty performed some kind of miracle with butterfly clips, since there wasn't enough flesh round the wound to facilitate stitches, and he worked very quickly, probably because he had been silly enough to inquire how the accident had happened – number one son was immediately in full spate. He managed, after a couple of days, to return to the lake by way of wearing bedroom slippers and bribing his brother to carry all the gear. They find a way, no matter what.

Another time we had spent a pleasant day beside a lake some twenty miles from home. Fairly uneventful, despite a few tench being caught and I began to wonder if the 'tench's curse' might not be a figment of a writer's fevered imagination.

However, at dusk the eldest caught yet another smallish tench and while shaking his hands free of slime and excess water after helping the creature to swim away, post photo session, he flicked his 'family heirloom', gold plated on silver, signet ring into the lake. It was great-grandfather's ring, beyond price in sentimental value. There followed a stunned silence as he stood perfectly still for several seconds before walking into the water, fully clothed and waist deep, in order to retrieve it – a seemingly impossible task. The lake bed was of silt and the trampling of size twelve army boots did nothing for the clarity of the water.

We resigned ourselves to a long wait because number one son is like his mother, stubborn and determined; he had already told us that there was no way he was leaving without it – and we believed him.

'Come out of there, David,' I called anxiously from the bank. 'It's only a piece of metal.' And, in desperation when there was no response, 'I'll buy you another one. Diamonds, platinum, anything. Just come out of the water!'

'I don't want another one,' he muttered. 'I'm going to get it back if it takes all night.' By a kind of miracle, after about twenty minutes spent groping in the silt, arms performing a sweeping motion, he found it and triumphantly held it aloft, like Excalibur from the waves, as he stepped soggily ashore. He told me afterwards that he hadn't picked the ring up. It had felt, he said, as if someone had placed in on the tip of his finger. Gave me the cold shivers, I can tell you.

I know from experience that I shouldn't get excited and start packing up, even though at least one of us needed a hot bath and a change of clothes. This session was no exception, for the turbulence caused by the disturbance to the lake bed had stirred up the silt and provided cover for the inquisitive tench who emerged tentatively in droves to find out what on earth that creature was, who had so rudely invaded their territory.

They were still visible, however, despite the cloudiness of the water and there were some *big* ones in there. All anglers, but particularly those under twenty, will endure any magnitude of discomfort to achieve their dream of breaking the tench record and I found myself praying that it would be soon, before he caught pneumonia instead.

Fortunately tench are not stupid. They drew straws so that, after half an hour, one of the larger of their number was caught and replaced, thus enabling them to enjoy a bit of peace and quiet as we finally packed up and trudged wearily in the direction of the car park. The journey home, as usual, was full of verbal action replay, concentrated mainly on the size and fighting ability of the seven-pound volunteer. Take my tip. Avoid tench expeditions if you can.

Trout for Tea

Trout fishermen wear funny hats, an essential part of the trout enthusiast's equipment, which are sometimes studded with hooks disguised by imitation flies with strange-sounding names.

My Chief Angler has been trout fishing only a few times but one particularly memorable occasion was an invitation, by a wealthy friend, to fish the River Test for the weekend.

'You don't mind if I go, do you?' begged Hubby. 'We'll have to rough it on the river bank, there's a small lodge apparently, but there'll be four of us so it won't be very comfortable.'

He went, of course, and I found out afterwards that the 'lodge' was fully furnished with all mod cons, down to a TV, video, hi-fi, fully stocked bar, microwave and freezer – some lodge! He was made to practise on a tributary for a few hours before being introduced to the resident Test trout. It is, he told me, considered to be unsporting if a trout is caught after the fly has been allowed to dip below the surface of the water and so the seasoned trout anglers had to make sure that he had

developed sufficient skill to fly fish in a gentlemanly manner. Smoked salmon and scrambled egg sandwiches, fresh strawberries and champagne were delivered to the riverside at lunchtime, so that they didn't have to stop their stalking of grayling and brown trout for too long, and they ate a several course meal in the local pub in the evenings. He decided that he could get to like trout fishing given a few more of these weekends.

The average trout angler, though, haunts lesser rivers and reservoirs, with only a cheese roll for company – although they do usually end up in a pub at the end of the day. Avoid them if they've had more than a couple of pints. This is when they get to the stage of repetitive conversation and you may find yourself cornered for hours at a time listening to phrases that make no sense at all as they show you the contents of their hats.

'That's a Tupp's Indispensable,' they'll tell you when

you indiscreetly ask them why the flies are all different. 'And that one's a Greenwell's Glory. I caught a seven pounder on this one – a Royal Coachman.'

It's best, at this point, to change the subject if you can. There are several dozen flies hooked into the hat and he will have a story of conquest for each and every one. You'll be stuck with him all evening if you don't escape.

Trout fishing is a fascinating sport to watch from the FW's point of view. At least there's some action involved instead of just an immobile float to gaze at – and trout is wonderful to eat – when they can be caught.

If you are fortunate enough to live within reasonable proximity to a trout farm – the ones where the proprietor provides you with a rod and trout pellets and the fish jump out of the pool and into your handbag – you could prepare the following gastronomic delight. If you can persuade your anglers to perform the necessary business, that is, for no self-respecting trout fisherman would be seen dead at a trout farm – there's no challenge if the fish are so keen to co-operate.

We visited a trout farm once, while on holiday in Somerset. Our visit lasted about fifteen minutes for we were only allowed to catch three trout for our entrance money. They would have been cheaper to buy in the local fishmongers but the excitement generated by my young son – then aged seven – when the imprisoned trout desperately fought to attach themselves to his hook, in the mistaken belief that anywhere was better than their overcrowded pond, was well worth the money.

Here's how to cook one, anyway, you never know your luck:

Stuffed Trout

This is virtually the same recipe as the one for sea bass on page 191, except that it is easier to get into the oven. I like to stuff the trout with a few chopped spring onions and a handful of button mushrooms and strew a few toasted almond flakes over the cooked fish, They will only take about 20 minutes in a hottish oven, and if you wrap them in tinfoil, prior to roasting, it means no washing up.

I've been hoping to meet, on a purely platonic plane, a dedicated trout fisherman who can't possibly consume all he catches. No luck, so far, all the trouters that I know seem to have a lot of friends already.

PART FOUR

The Sea Widow

Joys of Charter-boat Travel – Home and Away

The discomforts suffered aboard some boats can be indescribable although, I must admit, most charter-boats these days proudly boast of primitive toilet facilities. Not as primitive as some where there is no civilized place in which ladies may spend a penny. A bucket, strategically placed in the cabin is the most likely and this can be used only when the boat is anchored off – unless you know the skipper intimately and don't mind him fiddling with sonar devices or having ribald conversations on the ship's radio while you are answering nature's call.

The whole procedure is, in any event, undignified. Most anglettes/widows after a 'fun day out' wear jeans aboard boat. They are practical and warm but have the disadvantage of being extremely difficult to remove along with long johns, tights and knickers during cold spells and even more difficult to replace when the deed is done because you must hold on to the bucket at all costs. Even in a slight swell the boat will wobble precariously and skippers do not enjoy mopping up the cabin because you have stupidly let go of the bucket.

Attached to said bucket is a rope which you must hang on to for dear life both during and after swishing the bucket about in the sea. Let go of the rope and you cannot drink anything for the rest of the day. The men don't have to worry because they have outside plumbing anyway but the bucket is a concession made by the skipper especially for you. You should appear to be suitably grateful.

There isn't even a decent place to die in when the weather takes a turn for the worse. Nowhere to lie down and utter your last words. The deck is covered with unspeakable things awash in seawater and the cabin with its two 'emergency' bunks, reeks of fried bacon, sausages, onions, tomatoes, mushrooms, eggs and black pudding that the anglers ate for 'breakfast' at least twice in the last four hours. It's unwise to risk a nap on deck during sunlight hours, anyway. A red-haired friend of ours made this mistake and because he had lain on one side, he finished up resembling a block of coconut ice at the end of the day.

The worst part of the charter-boat day out, from the FW's point of view is the journey home when the anglers gut the catch of the day. They examine thoroughly the contents of each exposed stomach and make mental notes of what each specimen had for lunch – so that they can gather some of it during the week to tempt their prey the following weekend. The offal is thrown overboard where the seagulls grab it and scream avidly for more so, for about an hour, it can seem as if you are part of the set for an Alfred Hitchcock film.

The experienced fishing widow knows that the best way to deal with the boat weekends is to pack enough food for a regiment and send your anglers on their way – while you relax at home with a good book and a bottle or two of wine.

Mind you, the horrors of some British charter-boats are nothing compared to our European cousins' idea of a boat-fishing trip.

One member of our angling circle spends nearly half of his life abroad, his job demands it so he misses the local charter-boat trips. I'd go so far as to say he pines. So, when a colleague in his Belgium office suggested that he accompany the local fishing crowd on a boat trip one Sunday, he jumped at the chance. Everything would be taken care of, he was told. There would be no need to put himself out in the slightest. Bait would be provided, food for the day catered for and he could borrow all the gear since he had left his own precious tackle at home in England.

The day dawned, a bit breezy together with fine drizzle but they had arranged to meet in a local bar at 4 am – they never close, apparently – along with fifty or so other folk, none of whom spoke a word of English.

After a half-an-hour wait, fifty-eight eager, bright-eyed anglers loaded on to a coach for the two-hour journey to Ostend, during which time various raffles were held which our friend dutifully bought tickets for – he didn't win anything, needless to say.

Just before their arrival in Ostend, a further raffle was held and Kevin's name was called out first. 'Great,' he thought. 'At last I've won something,' and stood up prepared to collect his prize. Turned out that this raffle was to determine the order in which the anglers would embark – first called chose the best spots aboard ship.

Ostend docks at 6.30 am on a windy and freezing cold morning are not the best place to form an orderly queue but this is exactly what they did, beside the gangplank of a 160-foot trawler, as they waited for their names to be read out.

The most strategic place, decided our hero, was by the wheelhouse, especially as, by this time, the breeze had graduated to stiff-ish. The wind speed would have guaranteed, in this country, to deter any sane skipper from venturing on to the high seas or, at the very least, to consult the weather forecast. Not in Belgium.

The borrowed tackle consisted of a six-foot boat rod and a fixed spool reel which presented a challenge in itself, since Kevin had rarely used one. He began to yearn for his trusty old multiplier back in the garage of his suburban home. At least the bait was wrapped well. He opened his package and found five worms, all about a foot long – to last him for the day. His colleague explained that it was customary to cut off one-inch segments at a time. He was not to worry. There was no problem. The bait would last all day.

The lock seemed to take an eternity to fill up but, two hours later, there they were out on the open seas in a howling gale surrounded by forty-foot waves and with fifty-odd anglers, predominantly male but there were a couple or three females too, crammed into the cabin area buying bottled Belgian beer for breakfast.

After three hours, when they were sixty miles out, the weather began to deteriorate. Now there was a fifty- to sixty-foot swell. They decided it was time for lunch. Belgian lunch. Mostly cooked meats, sausages and bread. Suddenly, half way through this repast a horn sounded and all the anglers threw down their sandwiches – as opposed to throwing up their sandwiches, which is what they did later – and rushed to the same side of the boat where a huge wave promptly soaked everyone. The klaxon heralded permission to start fishing. Well, not exactly. It told the seasoned anglers that fishing was *about* to start. It also told our Kevin nothing at all but he sensibly watched everyone else and copied their actions. He soon discovered that the reason they were all on the same side of the boat was because they would have to drift fish, the weather being too rough to anchor up. The anglers, on hearing the second blast, were expected to prepare their tackle in readiness for the third sound of the horn, which would tell them to cast in. The fourth and final horn emission told them when to reel in.

Meanwhile, the waves were getting higher and higher, the wind, stronger and stronger. It was far too rough to fish and Kevin had had enough several hours ago. He couldn't find his workmate, whose raffle ticket had drawn a place far down the side of the boat but, he found out afterwards, the skipper had been approached by other less hardy anglers who had pleaded to be returned to shore. He steadfastly refused. They don't get paid, you see, until they have been at sea for a set number of hours and that time had not yet been reached.

The skipper did, however, relent sufficiently to take them inshore a bit. Two hours' motoring in took the waves down to only a thirty-foot well, and it was only raining monsoonish while the wind was 'blowing a hooligan'. The anglers were catching the occasional whiting, but only now and again and when Kevin, who had by this time used only half a worm, thought 'Sod it' and decided to use the remaining four and a half worms all on the same hook, his European shipmates though he was crazy.

Over the side went the hooked bait, with difficulty for Kev was trying to retain his balance and you need two hands to cast out, and after a few minutes there was a knock on the rod. He struck and was overjoyed to see his first bent rod of the day.

All at once and before he realized quite what was happening, the skipper, while yelling in Flemish, grabbed the line and began to hand pull it in leaving Kevin to reel up the slack. On the end of the line was a six-pound cod – along with four other lines belonging to adjacent anglers. Skip pulled it over on to the deck, cut the line and then wandered off, whereupon an unknown Belgian dived upon the fish, unhooked it, clasped it to his bosom and disappeared, only to materialize ten minutes later to return the cod. He had, so he said in Flemish, thought it was his since one of the lines attached to Kevin's hook had belonged to him. Of course, our hero didn't find out all these details until later when his friend translated for him – at the time, the poor bloke was totally mystified.

Kevin had now run out of bait but at last they started on the three-hour trip towards dry land. Once landed they all trooped back on to the coach ready for the homeward journey. The coach stopped two hundred yards from the docks, outside a chip shop where they had to queue for an hour to be served before being compelled to consume their supper in the street for no food was allowed on the coach.

They eventually made it home at 1 am – nearly a twenty-four hour trip in gruesome conditions, and the Belgians do it every weekend, regardless of the weather. And they think we British are nuts!

Back in the office, just a few hours later on Monday morning, the colleague asked our angler if he would like to join the club. I can't tell you his reply. It's unprintable but, he told me, never again would he complain about conditions aboard a British charter-boat.

Do You Know This Man?

Some fishing books I've read include an analysis of the type of person that takes up sea angling, purely from a male point of view but, as every fishing widow knows, there is another story.

The Gourmet: when you have slaved in the kitchen for two days in order to treat the 'lads' to a post-fishing-holiday dinner party – he's the one who says 'That was a beautiful meal, darling, but maybe a touch more garlic in the strawberry shortcake next time.'

The Winner: this chap has entered every competition within a three-hundred mile radius. He will pin you into a corner and insist that you listen to a myriad of tales of how, when and where he caught record weight specimens. Or put another way – what he threw over the side at any particular venue and which species was daft enough to bite the bait.

The Loser: he is just unlucky. It's not that he hasn't a clue how to catch fish, more that the fish have a vendetta against him and deliberately bypass his succulent bait and attach themselves to the hook of the bloke next to him.

The Boaster: whatever size fish is caught by his mates, this one has always caught, in some dark and distant past, a bigger specimen, but was too modest to have it weighed, witnessed and admired so there is no evidence – but 'Would I lie to you?'

The Skipper: skippers of charter-boats are a breed apart. Not only do they ramble on about the various aspects of the piscatorial art but you have to endure descriptions, at great length, of piston rings, bilge pumps and the latest sonar devices. At least he knows what he is talking about, unlike the next category.

The 'I Could Be a Skipper If I Wanted To': he knows more than the skipper. He knows where the best marks are although nothing is ever caught there. He goes to the Boat Show every year and gens up on the latest gadgets, foretells the weather regardless of the professional meteorologists' opinions, who in his view never get it right – and he wears a skipper's cap with scrambled egg on the peak.

The Croesus: all the most expensive fishing gear but next to no angling talent. Designer waders, green waxed cotton smocks and a huge gold ingot carefully draped outside the flotation suit. Drives this year's Mercedes, windows open in all weathers, radio on full blast but once aboard the boat catches nothing but crabs all day.

The Joker: he telephones at the crack of dawn and does a spot of heavy breathing, asks you what colour knickers you are wearing and do you happen to have a tide-table handy so he can calculate how many soft-backed crabs he can kidnap before the tide comes in.

The Landlord: every fishing fraternity has one of these. He's the proprietor of the local pub who knows that the post-mortem of every angling trip takes hours. He cunningly lays on sandwiches, crisps and peanuts thereby encouraging the anglers to stay on and spend even more money when they should be at home filleting the catch of the day.

The David Bailey: owns a camera with automatic everything on it. Rarely catches anything, he's too busy snapping. Every movement of everyone's cast and reeling in is on film. He always 'just happens' to have a few dozen photos of dead fish about his person at any given time.

The Sexist: insists that all female anglers are lesbians, especially if they catch more than he does, but he's always the one who gropes them in the pub after the match.

The Fishing Widow: when not spotted entering divorce courts, can be seen occasionally hanging around wharves and landing piers waiting for the tide to come in. More usually noticed sitting in groups in the corners of public bars with glasses of stagnant orange juice in front of them. They have to drive home – their anglers, having been drinking lager all day are by now well into the Blue Label vodka and unable to hold an unrepetitive conversation, let alone negotiate a Fiesta around corners.

The Karate Kid: after several pints threatens to 'duff up' anyone who disagrees with his description of the one that got away. Goes out for a wee and returns dusting himself down after having laid out three or four imaginary dissenters in the car park.

The Geriatric: this ageing angler is sympathetically tolerated by the younger versions, some of whom are not that much younger anyway. He fishes in the summer sun but in the winter when the arthritis sets in, he just goes along for the ride and the comradeship, offering constant advice which is acknowledged but largely ignored.

The Boy Angler: perfect clones of their fathers, these miniature aspiring fishermen are nothing more than a pain in the neck and various other parts of the anatomy to their sires. They ask 'stupid' questions every few seconds, have to be disentangled from assorted rigs and anchor chains, 'borrow' anything that isn't nailed to the deck, have to be fed, watered, kept warm, and generally behave in an inconsiderate and irresponsible manner.

The Can't Beat 'Em, Join 'Em: usually female, she may be present solely to prevent a 'boy angler' from being lashed to the mast by his father, but more probably, in the throes of young love, she is under the misapprehension that her presence will be noticed or even appreciated.

She would be better unnoticed. Any attempt to appear remotely glamorous in a Force 4 to 5 veering easterly requires a strong stomach and a steady hand with the lipstick. She will disembark at the end of the day with crystalline hair – the result of salt spray, or thirty-foot waves, on hair lacquer – and resembling a slightly inebriated giant panda – an effect of sea travel and non-waterproof mascara.

The Novice: he has no knowledge whatsoever about any aspect of fishing but all his mates have told him how great it is so he thinks he'll have a go. He can't touch the worms or cut up strips of herring; if he does he wants to wash his hands – with soap and fresh water – after every bait-up attempt. It has been known for an old hand to lend rod, reel, line and hook to a novice. Then bait the hook, cast out to sea, mention at the appropriate time that maybe the reason the rod is knocking so violently is that there could be a fish on the end of it. Instruct on methods of playing and reeling in, eventually take over when the going gets rough, gaff the captured prize and haul it aboard. Guess who receives the plastic trout on a wooden stand with 'Biggest Cod of the Century' written on it? You've got it – A NOVICE ESQ.

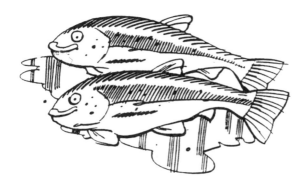

Blessed With Junior Anglers?

It is relatively easy to cope with infant or junior sea anglers – they are only too grateful to be allowed to join in and will do as they are told – until they reach their teens, that is.

They will prefix every sentence with 'Why?' and ask awkward questions like 'Why does the wind blow?' or 'Why is water wet?' but racking your brain cell in an effort to answer these little gems – and they won't be fobbed off, you have to come up with some kind of explanation – is a small price to pay when you consider the horrors you will have to deal with when they grow up.

All anglers have a mental age of about fourteen in their attitude towards their sport and the obsession reaches its peak at around this age. Rarely does it diminish but remains at the same intensity throughout their lives.

If you are planning a family it is a good idea to arrange to have your babies, as soon as possible, one after the other and although this is hard work in the early years it pays off later when they can both/all go fishing together in the school holidays. Otherwise you will have at least one of them whining at home that 'It's not fair, why won't he/they take me too?' If you already have your complement of children, then it is too late and you will have to put up with it.

Unfortunately your Chief Angler will be at work during most of the school vacations so you will be the one who has to put worms on hooks, deal with infant lacerations and remove the fish from the line when they do eventually manage to hook one by accident. It is no use telling your young ones that Daddy will take them fishing at the weekend. He won't. He will be too involved with his own fishing trip to spare the time and patience needed to instruct his quite small children.

As they grow bigger your Chief Angler will show a bit more interest and quite enjoy imparting his wisdom and expertise but by this time the youngsters want to go off on their own and resent being told what to do and how to do it.

Your teenagers will almost certainly find a soul-mate at school who is harbouring the same obsession to his bosom and they will commandeer the telephone for long periods when they organize a trip to a bit of coastline, some ten miles away from home.

On the day, you must make sure that you have thought of everything that they might need. Ask probing questions, go through the list of tackle that they will require and ensure that they have sufficient supplies of food and drink to last them eight hours. If you have teenage boys you will know that they need a rucksack or two just for sandwiches, let alone all the paraphernalia for a spot of angling.

Make absolutely certain that they have their bait. There is nothing more frustrating than driving your little treasures ten miles to the sea, only to be told when you arrive that the bait has been left on the kitchen table and must be collected and delivered with all speed by you, while they set up camp, otherwise what is the point of sitting on the shore all day? You have no choice even though this fishing trip has cost you several pounds for petrol, not to mention the wear and tear on the car and the gradual inflammation of your, as yet unsuspected, gastric ulcer.

They will have inherited the gene from their father which enables them to venture forth into the wilderness in all weathers. Be prepared for damp telephone calls requesting a lift home from an extremely muddy encounter with a couple of small flounders. Invest in a large roll of polythene which you can hurl over the car interior before you respond to this entreaty – you'd be surprised how far mud and sand can travel even when you think it is safely enclosed in the back seat.

If it is a boat-fishing trip – there are junior angling clubs who organize such days out – stock up on the chip supply for they will insist on eating their catch for supper. On the odd occasion when they catch nothing you can give them an egg or two with the chips by way of consolation while moppng up their tears of disappointment and listening to the story of how it got away – again.

When they win a competition it makes all the running about and worrying worth while for they may present you with a tea service or a bottle of Scotch while they proudly clutch the trophy which will stand, gathering dust, on the mantelpiece in their bedroom for a while until it is kicked under the bed during a game of 'Suffocate my brother with a pillow'.

It could be worse – at least while they are occupied in trying to capture the entire piscatorial kingdom they are not out mugging old aged pensioners or trying to get into pubs by lowering their voices a couple of octaves.

Make the most of it, soon they will be fully-fledged anglers and your troubles will begin in earnest.

Conger
Time

The conger eel season is preceded by a short period of relative calm for there's a lot of planning and preparation involved. Electrical appliances still suffer untold misery, as they do in most fishing households, but this should be expected and occurs all the year round regardless of the species currently in favour.

Vacuum cleaners fade away and die after a constant diet of lead weights, barbed hooks, 30lb breaking-strain line, swivels and the occasional elastic band. Washing machines die of broken hearts, not to mention bunged-up pumps, and hairdriers overheat to lay inert and gasping after being thrust down a wader leg in an attempt to dry out a bootfull of seawater in a hurry. When you have experienced a couple of conger seasons, however, you will be able to look upon all these mishaps as minor inconveniences.

The annual British Conger Club Championships are the highlight of the year and are heralded by the inexplicable disappearance of the only decent pair of secateurs that you possess. These are ideal for cutting up the bits of redundant lead jealously hoarded all year by the

Chief Angler's pet builder.

There ensue mysterious telephone conversations that are cut short the moment you walk into a room and I must warn you at this point – if your birthday or wedding anniversary falls in the summer months, don't be deceived into thinking that your Chief Angler is planning a surprise for you. You will get a surprise, certainly, but don't get dressed up for it.

At some point, molten lead will appear in the best saucepan and neat but solid trails will be laid across the kitchen units when the weight-construction and lager-drinking evenings are under way. You will suffer a pounding headache and lightheadedness from inhaling the lead fumes and be bribed with numerous cups of coffee to stay out of the kitchen. Makes a dead Hoover pale into insignificance, let me tell you.

Some time in July a mountain of fishing gear is loaded into the van along with a small suitcase containing several pairs of underpants and a toothbrush. They're off! For a whole week with the conger eels in Brixham. Even the Hoover perks up a bit.

For a few days life is blissful. The house has no strange, hidden aromas. The phone stops ringing. You do not notice whether the tide is in or out and if a stiff breeze springs up it just means that you can get the washing dry.

By the end of the week, though, withdrawal symptoms will have set in and you will begin to miss the cameraderie and good-natured bickering of the fishing crowd.

They will arrive home exhausted and unshaven but bearing gifts – a couple of sticks of rock, a case brimful of dirty washing and 'It's all on video'.

A word of warning about the video. On no account must you allow it to be shown in front of respectable

neighbours, children under fourteen or anyone of a nervous disposition. The anglers begin filming on their best behaviour and are a little camera conscious but, as the excitement mounts and bigger and bigger congers are caught, even the most gentle and well-bred of the angling party can be heard screaming obscenities and it can be quite shocking if you are a new FW.

It's all worth while, though, for occasionally they will catch a monster and your angler will be famous for a week – until one of the crowd gets a bigger one.

Fun For All

Having been regaled for several years with the delights and fascinations of conger fishing in Brixham, it was decided, in a vague and patronizing kind of way, that we would be allowed to accompany the fishing party for a weekend. Not the whole week, you understand, for this might seriously disrupt the conger programme.

There were conditions: we must share a suitcase otherwise there would not be room for all the tackle in the minibus and we were to 'amuse ourselves' all day and only meet up with our anglers in the evenings for a meal. No late nights or discos – they would have to be aboard at 4 am and therefore needed their sleep. We were not to get in the way.

The July morning that we left was the first day of the monsoon season which we drove through, leaving extensive flooding to right and left behind us.

On arrival in Brixham, some five hours later, for we only stopped once on the way for ten minutes, to visit the loo and to drink a hurried (or should I say horrid) cup of coffee – a double negative action if ever I saw one – the weather was very, very warm and humid but hardly any rain to speak of.

Our driver, normally a careful and fairly considerate road-user, for a man, pulled across the road with almost total disregard of the inconvenience caused to the rest of the early morning traffic and ground to a shuddering halt outside the hotel entrance.

Within ten minutes the contents of the minibus had been hurled into various bedrooms, the bus parked in the multi-storey car park across the street and they were off, hurtling merrily down to the harbour wall, leaving the FWs to unpack the unimportant items such as clothes and toilet requisites.

My elder son, on being told that he must unpack his own suitcase promptly opened a wardrobe door, up-ended his open case into it and declared himself ready for the fray. It only took him thirty seconds and I was too exhausted to argue.

After surveying the harbour and satisfying them-selves that the sea, sky and fishing boats were still there and all functioning as they should, the anglers gravitated purposefully towards the Rising Sun, in order to 'discuss tactics for tomorrow'. This discussion took over three hours and considerable amounts of alcohol so we FWs looked round the innumerable gift shops and mentally spent about fifty pounds each on rubbish to take home to our friends and families, before returning to the hotel to await our befuddled menfolk.

In Brixham, and I asssume all the coastal resorts of South Devon, there live megalithic seagulls. Their rau-cous cries can be heard continually, night or day and I swear we had one flying past our bedroom window crying out for help – which he appeared to need all night. We saw one bird with a piece of string trailing from his beak – obviously some desperate but enter-prizing individual had tried to tie its mouth up and failed. These gulls will eat anything – pickled-onion-flavoured crisps, the chocolate bits from the bottom of Cornettos – even clotted-cream toffees thrown to maim and seaside rock aimed to kill.

They even had a go at a couple of used teabags which one of our party threw in exasperation. When we asked one of the boat skippers how the local people stood the incessant noise of the sea birds, he said – in that wonderful Devon dialect that I could listen to for hours – 'Oi carn 'ear nuthern, moi luverr,' so maybe one becomes accustomed eventually but, let me tell you, it takes longer than a weekend.

The following morning we fishing widows booked ourselves on to the ferry from Brixham to Torquay and 'amused ourselves' on the journey by watching one of our group turning various shades of green. We were not certain whether her colourful condition was due to mild seasickness or our conversation at the time, a discussion of an Ann Summers party which one of the girls had attended in a vain attempt to lure her man from the deep.

On arrival at Torquay, which incidentally I had assumed was Paignton until enlightened after about an hour, we visited a palmist on the pier, who was so accurate with her preternatural summary of my past that I almost believed her when she said she could predict that we would one day run a guesthouse or a pub in the West Country.

Was she kidding, or what? Who did she think would be doing all the work while 'they' would be out trying to catch fish 'for the table'. I was in such a state of shock that one of the girls bought me a huge ice cream to calm me down. She ate one herself and declared it to be positively orgasmic. Seeing my surprise at her remark, she told me to be realistic. 'Which, given the choice, would you prefer, Rosie?' she asked. 'Especially after they have been on a fishing boat for twelve hours or more.' I could see what she meant immediately and ate my cornet deep in profound thought.

Later that afternoon we were ferried back to Brixham, this time watching our aforementioned friend turn from a healthy pink through grey to white but we were discussing the wedding of one of our party to one of their party at the time, enough to make anyone change colour.

We sat on the wharf to await the imminent arrival of our anglers. We waited for two and a half hours.

When the boat eventually came in we waited until they had unloaded the fish, weighed the big ones and had a quick pint or several in the pub before we could go back to the hotel to eat and listen to the post-mortem on the poor creatures they had outwitted and murdered during the day.

The journey home was too soon after the journey away and we were all suffering from minibus lag by the time we returned, but they said we can all go again next year if we behave ourselves. I must save up for a few of those ice cream cones.

Brixham
Revisited

We went again this year. Along with the lead weights and conger traces, we were allowed to go again. We left home at 1.30 am because I had to drive and He thought we'd better allow plenty of time to get there, seeing as how I've no sense of direction and am pretty generally useless anyway.

Travelling all night through the dark bits of the motorway, and unexpected patches of dense fog, is not guaranteed to get you into holiday mood. We stopped once at a motorway services for the usual desperate wee and hurriedly ingested cup of coffee and they promised us a sumptuous breakfast on arrival at our destination, if only we would get a move on.

At 7 am, this wonderful meal was served on very thick china plates, in transport-cafe-type surroundings but it was very nicely cooked and cheap, if not exactly living up to the promise of the kedgeree and devilled kidneys which my imagination had savoured all the way from South Mimms.

After breakfast, and we were thankful that they had allowed us to eat first – probably to avoid the inconvenience of our prostrate-with-hunger bodies littering up the sea wall – we were frog-marched down to the wharf and forced to watch a local pensioner mackerel bashing for an hour, until the hotel promised to show signs of life – and let me tell you that eggs, bacon and fried bread does not mix particularly well with the smell of diesel fumes and stale conger juice from moored fishing boats.

In due time, as we hovered expectantly outside the hotel we were rewarded by the opening of the main door and the exodus of another fishing party. There was so much tackle and luggage on the pavement that our large sailbag, full to the brim with oilskins, thermal underwear and other vital commodities, became 'misplaced'. By the time this dire catastrophe was discovered, the other party was half way to Wales so frantic lists were drawn up of the necessary purchases that must be made, that same morning, as soon as the shops opened.

We had fish and chips for dinner that night, and fish and chips the next night, after They had come in from a good day's fishing. And they actually went into the hotel first to have a wash and change their clothes.

The following night we had fish and chips for dinner, only this time they were too tired to wash and change. The stench of three-day-old fishing smocks coupled with the fact that the fish restaurant was extremely cosy – we were crammed together like sardines, appropriately enough – did nothing for the flavour of our cod and chips.

We wouldn't have minded if we never ate fish and chips again and spoke sharply to our anglers resulting in the promise of a decent meal at Chandler's on the following evening.

This promise, which we took with a pinch of salt – as

is wise to consider all promises made by anglers in the throes of a post-mortem discussion, they'll say anything just to shut you up – was unexpectedly kept. Not with very good grace, I might add. They objected quite strongly to the obligatory wash, shave and clean knickers and my Chief Angler had the anguish of a broken rod to contend with, but we convinced them that it would be well worth the effort.

Chandler's is a respectable restaurant and the food is cooked to a very high standard. I've eaten in many establishments and can honestly say that this place is one of the best and, as a bonus, the lady of the house has a lively sense of humour about which more later.

The next day, after our menfolk had left in search of eels, our boat skipper's wife very kindly gave up her valuable time and took us to some of the local tourist attractions – one of which was Kents Cavern. This complex of Stone-Age caves was a lot less horrifying than I had imagined. I suffer from claustrophobia and was frankly terrified before I went in. Such was my relief on emerging once more into the civilized and daylight world that I handed over, without a qualm, sufficient money for my fourteen-year-old son to buy an inflatable green dinosaur which was immediately baptized with Coca-Cola and named Dennis. Dennis proved to be an investment although I didn't know it at the time.

Our anglers seemed to be coming in later and later each evening. Towards the end of the week we stood on the wharf as usual waiting for our menfold when Joy gave a sudden yelp and put her hand to her hip, she said it felt as if someone had hit her. Someone had – a friendly seagull had left her a present, covering one side of her cream linen skirt. God only knows what this creature had consumed for its lunch but, judging by the mess, it must have been at least a large Vindaloo followed by prunes and custard. I thought all birds' droppings were of the white variety that are so difficult to remove from car windscreens, but this was almost human. Poor Joy was so worried that people might think she was the incontinent one that we hurried back to the hotel so that she could wash and change.

We waited for our friend in the hotel bar and by the time she had washed both herself and the skirt, we had decided to stay where we were and wait in comfort for our anglers to stumble in whenever they felt like it.

By this time it was dark and a bit chilly so we felt that we were in the best place. Not for long. One of the locals came into the bar with his wife, presumably for a pre-prandial drink, spotted us three FWs and began to make phallic gestures in our direction with his right forearm. Unable to believe what we were seeing we thought, at first, that maybe he'd had an accident, poor chap, and was exercising his arm. We tried to ignore him but he was not the kind of man to be disregarded so we stayed silent as he pulled up a stool and seated himself at our table. His long-suffering wife was still up at the bar and she had all our sympathy, for she was obviously used to his behaviour. After several attempts to shock us with four-letter words, which we had all heard before from our anglers in post-match discussions, he started to become irritated because there was no typically feminine reaction to his efforts.

Meanwhile, Simon, who was going through the 'protective towards his mother' stage, spotted what was going on from his vantage point by the window and crept over to my side clutching his inflated Dennis the Dinosaur. Unfortunately for Dennis his head and neck are reminiscent of a willy and of course our over-sexed companion spotted this immediately.

'Which one of these lovely ladies is your Mum?' he

asked my son. No answer.

'Well, whichever one of them it is, boy. You tell her that I've got one of them,' pointing at Dennis's upper regions, 'in between my legs. I'll show her how it works, anytime.'

By this time, Simon had deflated Dennis and quick as a flash came back at our friend with 'What? Green and flat do you mean?'

The other locals in the bar, who had been listening avidly to the whole conversation, yelled and clapped as we watched Casanova's ego deflate to an echo of Dennis. He grabbed his wife and left as my son was given all the Coca-Cola he could drink, peanuts, crisps, money, promises of undying devotion and all his own way for the rest of the week.

We were almost at the end of our week, anyway. The last evening was to be a celebration, with a sumptuous dinner at Chandler's, in honour of the qualification for entry to the British Conger Club of our two youngest

anglers. We sent our conger hunters off in the morning for their last day at sea and spent the rest of the day sorting ourselves out in anticipation for the evening.

The table was booked for nine o'clock thus giving them plenty of time, we thought, to get suited and booted or at least washed and shaved. They said they'd be back by seven at the latest but it is always best, to avoid disappointment, to add an hour on to the time that they promise to be anywhere.

Anyway, we thought we were on a winner and went into Chandler's that afternoon for a complacent cream tea – the penultimate of the holiday treats. We paid for the cream tea but asked the owner's wife to add the amount on to the bill in the evening, as a joke – just to see if any of the menfolk would spot it.

Well, they waited until we were all showered, painted and perfumed and had donned the 'just in case we get to go out in the evenings' frock – and then they telephoned from the boat.

'We're sorry,' they said. 'We're going to be later than we thought. You'd better go ahead without us. We'll get there when we can.'

We did, although none of us felt much like eating by this time – more like enduring life imprisonment for murder. Anyway, we ate and paid the bill after explaining the situation to our hostess, who naturally wanted to know why we were unescorted on the last evening.

As we were leaving, Madame Chandler suggested that we tell our anglers that we had eaten but not paid the bill and they would have to settle it up in the morning before we left.

'I'll give you a bill that will knock their socks off,' she said.

We appeared to have consumed four of everything on the menu – including four bottles of the finest red wines, eight brandies, plus the most expensive cream tea in Christendom. The bill for four of us – including my fourteen year old who drank water – came to £204.42.

When our menfolk eventually tumbled into the hotel bar where we were waiting with gin and tonics unconsumed in front of us – we'd been drinking Perrier until we saw the whites of their eyes – they were so guilt-ridden that they would have agreed to anything. So, when we gave them the restaurant bill they gulped a bit but didn't say much else. My eldest son spoilt it all, for we were going to let them stew until the following morning, or at least count their remaining cash to see if they could afford our meal.

'What are crevettes, Mum?' he asked, going through the bill with a toothcomb. He's always hungry and very interested in food, even if it's only seeing what other people have had for their dinner. Like a fool I'd forgotten to ask and not being absolutely certain that they were prawns and also being a terrible liar I couldn't think of anything convincing to say.

They were more upset because they had fallen for our ruse than if they had been called upon to pay the bill, but at least we had a few moments of triumph, and we did go out and try to get fish and chips for them. Too late, naturally, because by the time the inquest was over, the cafes and even the fast-food places had all closed. Luckily, Alice, our landlady, took pity on them and cooked them sausages, eggs and chips – not that they noticed what they were eating by this stage in the game – so they didn't have to go to bed hungry.

We've decided not to go next year. Well, we'll see it all on video when they come back, anyway. Several times.

Man Overboard

The lengths some anglers will go to in order to pursue their sport defies credibility – and it is supposed to be fun. A leisure pursuit.

Angling aboard a friend's boat in high summer can be very thirsty work, so they tell me, especially in the company of a crowd of mates whom they haven't seen since last weekend – there's so much to talk about – gives you a very dry throat, that does.

A nasty attack of 'barley wine', suffered in the wake of several hours of hot sun and sea air can have a devastating effect on the middle ear, or that's how anglers will claim to justify their unsteadiness. You must understand that it has nothing whatsoever to do with the alcohol content of their chosen thirst-quenching beverage. Sooner or later vertigo becomes a safe bet, resulting in the occasional bizarre casualty.

Jim Smith had hooked into a largish tope and was coping very well, under the barley-wine circumstances, until the tope decided that enough was enough and pulled the other way. Our hero lost what precarious balance he had and fell slowly, gracefully but inevitably, over the side, disappearing before his fellows into the deep – seemingly, never to be seen again.

They fished him out after he had bobbed to the surface for the third time, the delay being caused because the life-belt was buried under empty bottles and spent lager cans – *that* would never have been allowed on a charter-boat.

Jim was, so he said, none the worse for his unexpected swim and was still hanging on grimly to his rod, still hooked into the tope. He boated the fish first, before spitting out the excess sea water in his system and then had the nerve to complain about wasted fishing time as he attempted to dry out his clothes and the contents of his wallet.

At least he was safe, fit and well which cannot be said about another member of the circle. Our estuary has the usual rip currents running through it which can sweep you out to sea no matter how good a swimmer you are – even an Olympic champion would find it hard going. This particular angler was warned not to venture in for a dip, but he was from South Africa. Current? What current? He had swum around Durban harbour, many a time, with no ill effects and there are shark and barracuda in Durban harbour. He was hard, he had tattoos. No sweat.

He had been in the water for a good hour before he gave in and admitted defeat. Despite swimming strongly against the tide, he was gradually being swept farther and farther away from the boat but refused to lose face and ask for help from the rest of the angling party, who were shouting encouragement while falling about laughing, being sensibly aboard and enjoying every minute of the spectacle. Eventually, they took pity on the poor soul, threw him a line and hauled him aboard. He lay gasping and spewing up the best part of the Thames for quite a while before retiring to prostrate himself upon the emergency bunk in the wheelhouse, where he spent the rest of the day. It was several months before he could be persuaded to venture on to the high seas again and a number of years before his companions stopped asking him, at every opportunity, if he fancied a swim.

Bait-digging at night can be hazardous too, especially if you are not very tall. Several of our angling circle had braved the elements to harvest ragworm one evening, armed with Tilley lamps for lighting and the usual buckets and forks. By necessity they have to walk out the regulation distance from the shore before they can dig and this involves crossing a couple of creeks.

It was OK on the way out, the tide was still going out so the creeks were emptying. Unfortunately there was a freak tide that night, and the water turned earlier than expected so on the way back the creeks had filled up quite a bit. It can be dangerous if you get caught out by the tide. Our local coastguard is regularly called upon to rescue unsuspecting tourists who have become stranded on the sandbanks.

They crossed the first creek without mishap but by the time they arrived at the second one, it was almost full so they had to wade across it. One of the anglers is only five feet tall and, as they waded in crocodile file, hanging on to each other's shoulders, with Tilley lamps held aloft – he disappeared.

He was carried to safety, in pitch darkness because his companions were laughing so much that they had dropped the lamps in the water, thereby extinguishing their only source of light. It would have been cheaper to buy the few ragworm that they had managed to glean. The expense of several brandies which they had to pump into the little chap, to restore him to full working order, would have covered the cost of a couple of hundred worms.

'It's all part of life's adventure,' they will tell you when you question their sanity.

My Chief Angler is as bad as all the rest. One dark and misty November night the boat skipper calculated that the tide was not going to be high enough to cast off from the wharf. The boat was therefore anchored a couple of miles offshore in the Ray – a natural tidal gut-way, regularly dredged and where the water remains at a relatively constant depth.

There is a hard path, laid over the mud flats, which leads almost directly into the Ray, so that anyone wishing to reach the moored boats doesn't have to trudge stickily through acres of mud. Great. Until the tide doesn't come in quite far enough and the charter-boat skipper dare not creep any close to the shore area of the Ray, for fear of going aground.

My CA reached the end of the hard path and, seeing his goal in sight, began to wade across the shallows towards the boat, pulling up his waders as the water level grew higher. It slopped over the top of his thigh-length boots eventually, edged its way up to his waist, then chest deep but, with only a few yards to go and by carefully balancing his Shakespeare Box on top of his head, rods held aloft, he made it.

Once aboard he was forced to strip naked, and drape himself in a very itchy blanket, kindy provided by a smiling skipper and held in place with a belt. He wore this unconventional apparel all night and well into the next day because his clothes, sodden with salt water, refused to dry without the aid of a wintery sun and a brisk north-easterly. This strange mode of dress did not interfere with his day's sport, he told me. Such was the pace of the day that he didn't notice the whistling of the wind through his nether regions.

When, a couple of days later, he related his adventure to a long-distance angling friend, he was not asked if he was physically OK, if he had caught a chill or if he had suffered abrasions in unnatural places through fishing with no clothes on. No. You can guess the first question, can't you?

Did he catch anything?

No Sex Please, We're Anglers

The fact that anglers are able to procreate, to reproduce their own kind, must amount to one of the lesser miracles, given the unorthodox way in which most of them arrange their lives. They have a normal sex-drive – over-sexed, some of them – but their problem is time and tide. The old adage 'time and tide wait for no fishing widow' is very, very true.

There is a little romance in our lives, but not much. Not because our anglers don't have feelings, but because they have difficulty in fitting them in to the fishing programme. They should not be condemned or divorced for this, since they already suffer enough guilt to satisfy an Old Bailey jury.

Most sea anglers' babies are conceived during a howling gale or a blizzard – or occasionally in dense fog, if the charter-boat doesn't have radar fitted. There is an aid to normal contraception methods in angling relationships, look upon it as a bonus – or not – depending on your libido at the time. I'm talking about the frustration of telephone calls which occur just as you are reaching boiling point – they give a whole new meaning to 'coitus interruptus'.

If it's one of *your* friends your red-hot angler will beg

you to hurry up, to cut short your riveting conversation about whose turn it is to perform the school run on Monday or what strange ingredients a mutual friend has manufactured into jam. He loves you and can't wait to prove it.

More often than not though, it will be a fellow angler who is desperate to be informed of the latest bait situation and at what time the trip will start out from the wharf the following weekend. You will be cast aside while your angler gropes in the bedside cabinet drawer, where he just happens to keep a tide-table, and proceeds to discuss tactics, venues and the fickleness of the British climate. This can last for up to twenty minutes, by which time you will have gone off the boil, given up and commenced Hoovering the house from top to bottom in an attempt to gain some release from unquenched ardour.

Those of you who are involved with a mechanically minded angler will relate to the call that is received in the early hours of the morning. It will be from an apologetic but panic-stricken boat skipper who has just discovered a dodgy bilge pump or a wayward fish finder. Your man will rush down to the wharf, taking his tool box with him, to offer his services only to return, equally hurriedly, a couple of hours later to grab his tackle and run. The skipper, eternally grateful, will have invited your angler to accompany the fishing party for the day as payment for his help.

When an angler sires a son there is great jubilation in the fishing circle because the little mite is looked upon as a potential bait-digger. Fatherly minds move on rapidly, about fourteen years, and anticipate the time when they will be able to 'retire' and allow their collective offspring to gather the harvest of lugworm required for a joint fishing trip. They still wet the baby's head even if it's a girl, but the ceremony doesn't have quite the same intensity. Not many girls are willing to stand waist deep in mud, picking up worms with their bare hands – even for their beloved fathers.

Don't forget that the christening has to be held on a non-fishing weekend. Not only 'non-fishing' for your Chief Angler, but for the majority of the guests as well. Unless you make loud noises your baby could be attending secondary school before you get a Sunday that is convenient to everyone in your circle of angling friends and relations.

I know of one fishing widow who has seven sons who are all under ten years old. How she managed it remains a mystery to we less fertile fishing widows and, more to the point, so does how she has managed to retain her sanity this far. When his mates playfully asked the proud father if he was aiming for a football team, he denied it vehemently. He was going for a bait-digging syndicate and was most put out that his associates didn't realize the fact.

Don't make the mistake of getting excited when they come home with a butt pad and a harness. I know it looks like a marital aid and is mildly phallic when put on complete with rod butt, to try it for size, but that's as far as they go before replacing it lovingly in its box until the conger trips begin and you will only be disappointed.

Of course you could always anoint yourself with concentrated pilchard oil and await developments, but you've got to be desperate to try that one – it won't wash off and takes several days for the stench to fade sufficiently for you to leave the house without the risk of receiving anxious glances from passers by. How do I know? I'll give you three guesses.

Be patient, you will be rewarded eventually and let's

face it, if you are the type of woman who gets turned on by waders and oil-skins, and you must have been at one time or you wouldn't have tangled with them in the first place, you deserve all you get.

Skating on Thin Ice

There will be occasions when your anglers will catch a multitude of skate or thornback rays. Strangely, there doesn't appear to be a happy medium with the skate-hunting expeditions. They will either catch a couple of dozen or none at all. It seems such a terrible waste when they take out a stone of fresh, bright-eyed herring for bait and return empty-handed, having thrown all the herring, cut into succulent strips, over the side of a boat. It is possible to feed the family for a fortnight on what they throw into the sea.

As you can only force a certain amount into the freezer, the surplus catch has to be eaten or distributed to the neighbours. With a little imagination you can always give a dinner party using the remainder. You will find yourself trying to dream up a menu but skate will dominate your thoughts. You will be surrounded by it and the only dishes which spring to mind will be things like Skate Cocktail followed by Skate and Kidney Pie with Skate and Walnut Pudding for dessert – with custard.

This you will be able to get away with only if you

force-feed your visiting anglers with enough lager before the meal so that they become confused, not too difficult a task to accomplish, and if you turn the lights down low they won't know what they are eating anyway. Do not make the mistake of serving a dinner by candlelight to anglers – they will just assume that the lights have fused.

There is a disgusting old fisherman's tale about skate – and don't tell me that you don't know any disgusting old fishermen. There is at least one in every fishing fraternity. They say that the genitalia of these creatures (skate – not disgusting old fishermen) resemble that of human beings and, for this reason, bringing the whole fish ashore is prohibited. Only the wings are allowed in, the body, complete with dangly bits, is thrown overboard for the delectation of the sea birds, or it should be. My Chief Angler once brought home a whole, very well endowed roker which he left laying, in all its glory, on newspaper ready to be dealt with. My mother, who happened by before he could chop off the offending bits, pointed to the skate's generously proportioned protuberance and asked me what it was. I told her. She has never eaten skate since.

According to the wise old men of the sea, 'in the old days' the female skate were 'used' by desperate, deep-sea fishermen who had spent a great deal of time afloat on the briny without sight of a woman. Anything looks sexually attractive, they told me, after several months adrift with only the golden rivet for company. If, as I was before being graphically enlightened, you are too naive to know the significance of the golden rivet, let me just say that the cabin-boy was not always accommodating enough to bend over and search for it.

The story made me feel quite ill, the next thing you know there will be photos of skate sent into the 'men only' magazines, with black sticky tape over their eyes – under the heading of 'Readers' Skate'. Almost puts you off your food.

Fortunately our anglers are only at sea for an average of twelve hours at a time – mind you, there is always one pervert per charter-boat, so we shouldn't become too complacent.

To land these magnificent creatures is quite difficult, so I am told. It's a bit like flying a kite underwater. You can imagine the rays with wings outstreched, teeth gritted, pulling against the twenty-pound breaking-strain line for all they are worth – anything to avoid being caught by disgusting old fishermen. Fishing widows can only too readily relate to this.

Be prepared for plenty of bad language as your angler tries to remove the skin from skate. The only practical way is with a pair of strong pliers and brute strength. All the hard work pays off in the end though, because these fish are delicious if you cook them in butter, with loads of black pepper, and serve with new potatoes and salad. If you can prevent yourself from dwelling on the old fisherman's tale, that is. Try not to think about it. I'm sure it's only a legend.

Make That a Double

Bait-diggers, along with tackle-shop dealers, are revered by everyone connected to the angling fraternity – for different reasons. They are treated with respect and consideration at all times. Rarely do you see a bait-digger in a pub without a pint beside him which has been bought by an angler who has a competition next weekend and requires the juiciest and most succulent worms for himself. He may even run to a double Scotch if he's really keen.

These rewards are richly deserved for it's not the most comfortable job in the world, bait-digging. The worms and/or crabs have to be harvested in all weathers, exposing the fragile bait-digging bodies to sunburn or pleurisy, depending on the season.

There are occasions when all the effort of digging appears to have been a complete waste of time and energy because the weather forecasters have got it wrong again and a hurricane begins an hour before cast-off. The hard-earned worms may be dumped into the sea by unappreciative anglers, causing the bait-digger to cry into his beer.

There are other times when the tide doesn't go out at all so the poor bait-digger sits gloomily on the shingle, like Neptune but without the throne, waiting in vain for the retreat of the waters while mentally debating whether or not it would be worth while driving for a couple of hours to a place, farther round the coast, where the tide *has* gone out. They usually go – the punters must not be disappointed.

To the Foreshore Officers and other authorities bait-diggers are the scum of the earth. Hated and despised, they are frequently chased for several miles over the mud by red-faced, exhausted officialdom – it's hard work running through mud when you are not equipped with bait-digging 'go faster' wellies.

The reason for this persecution is not the fault of the bait-digger. The juiciest worms and most succulent soft-backed crabs are not stupid, they choose to set up house just a few yards on the wrong side of the 'legal digging line', forcing the conscientious bait-digger to break the law in order to fulfil his obligations to his many clients.

It can be a very risky business for if they are caught, and their foes invariably catch up with them sooner or later, they are charged with 'illegal digging of bait' and can be incarcerated in a cell for an hour or two – to teach them a lesson – until the powers that be decide that they appear sufficiently chastened to be deposited back into humanity. This is usually a couple of miles from their carefully and legally parked transport – and it's always seriously raining, or worse.

Added to these hazards and discomforts is the tedious job of sorting and caring for the creatures until they are needed. Tanks have to be cleaned out at intervals and aerating pumps debunged. The bait must be scrutinized every so often and dead worms or ailing crabs removed or resuscitated. Try giving a match angler a dead ragworm – the reaction is terrifying. The injured party will spread the word so that the reputation of the bait-digger becomes tarnished and that's not good for business.

So when the anglers scream 'How much?' when presented with their bait bill, although they may think it exorbitant, when you weigh up the toils of the trade and add on the expert local knowledge that a bait-digger must have before he can bait-dig successfully, it's worth every penny.

This expert local knowledge is of vital importance to a bait-digger. I know of one who took an angling friend with him on one of his forays when they trudged three miles and dug for a couple of hours, our professional explaining technique and giving of his expertise all the while. Admittedly the friend was still as high as a kite after a party the night before, but his three worms didn't go very far towards complementing the five hundred required by an anticipating customer.

Bait-diggers are beloved of fishing widows. Upon these wondrous specimens of manhood – and, I dare say, womanhood for there must be a few females out there too, although I don't personally know any women who would be insane enough to stand waist deep in mud and effluent just to please the angling fraternity – upon these special people rest the domestic harmony and marital bliss of many. I emphasize the marital bliss for who wants to go to bed with a man who is not concentrating on the job in hand but who is preoccupied and fretting over tomorrow's bait supply, or whether his waders will dry out in time for a trudge over the flats?

There is the odd perk for our precious bait-diggers now and again. They are chatted up or mothered, depending on their inclinations, by women of all ages and every description. They are invited to parties, weddings, christenings and the occasional funeral, generally made much of and rightly so. Bait-diggers contribute greatly towards their customers' enjoyment of a quiet life.

Christmas Afloat

Fishing widows have to cope with two Christmas celebrations every year. There is the usual one on 25 December but also, more importantly, the annual festive high jinks aboard the charter-boat.

Christmas on the high seas usually occurs over the weekend preceding the real one and needs just as much planning and organization – and more than a little ingenuity.

They hold 'a meeting' at the local pub to discuss and delegate the various Christmas components. They work out the cost and divide it equally so they all know how much they must put into the kitty, then one by one the anglers are sent off with their lists of things to buy and prepare. One sorts out the turkey – although one year they had pheasant and duck, courtesy of a gourmet who had decided that turkey was a little mundane, bearing in mind the eminence of the occasion. Another organizes the pudding, someone is in charge of the vegetables etc, but we fishing widows know who will really be on the business end of the preparation, don't we?

For obvious reasons everything has to be cooked in

The Sea Widow

advance – most charter-boats are only equipped with a small gas stove. The turkey can, at a pinch, be eaten cold and tinned potatoes, peas and carrots can be heated in one saucepan, but they will want bacon rolls, chipolatas and stuffing to go with it. You may have to invest in a couple of large, wide-necked vacuum flasks to accommodate these vital additions to their Christmas lunch. 'It won't be the same otherwise,' they'll tell you.

The trimmings for the turkey must be heated up at home, in the small hours of the morning, and wrapped in separate pieces of tinfoil after which you will have to force it into the cavities of the flasks and hope for the best. They will, on their return, complain that everything tasted OK but was of no recognizable shape. You can ignore their criticism because they will pass out, from a surfeit of Christmas spirits, shortly after uttering their displeasure and by the time they regain consciousness will have forgotten all about it.

They set off in the frost and gloom, full of joie de vivre and almost childish excitement in anticipation of the day ahead. They're armed with their Christmas dinner, a plastic bag containing mince pies and sausage rolls, a couple of boxes of crackers and pocket full of Christmas cards. Incidentally, the cards that you receive when they come ashore in the evening will have to be washed and dried before you can hang them anywhere in the house – and while on the subject of cleaning, avoid at all costs those aerosol cans of squirty cream to go with the Christmas pudding. Most of it ends up over their clothes during the squirty cream fight that seems to be a natural progression after the pudding has been consumed, and you will have a terrible few hours trying to remove it. Give them a couple of tins of custard instead.

There is a crate of lager waiting for them aboard the

boat and there will be bottles of rum, brandy and vodka 'to keep out the cold'. Someone will have a camera to record the event for posterity but, as the alcohol takes its toll, the pictures after lunch gradually lose their clarity and the last few prints on the film will be so out of focus, sideways or upside down that the photo lab will refuse to process them.

They wear paper crowns over their balaclavas and a Christmas tree has been lashed to the mast – complete with coloured fairy lights run off a twelve-volt battery. Tinsel has been threaded over the rails and through the gantry and a five-pound tin of chocolates is opened to be left in a convenient place for anyone who has the stomach for them. I haven't been able to find out if they hang up wader's socks and wait for Santa, no one will admit to it, but they come home with small gifts – a shiny bait knife, packets of hooks and the like, so it's

anyone's guess. Eventually they bait up and cast out.

The cod have no idea what they are letting themselves in for. Allowing themselves to be caught, just to see what all the noise and merriment is about, they are hauled over the side, clubbed to death and 'dressed'. You may receive a ten pounder wearing a paper hat with a motto in its mouth but only the biggest fish receive this honour, the smaller ones have to be content with a strip of tinsel round the belly – it's bizarre.

When it's all over for another year and you begin to prepare for the family festivities, don't expect any enthusiasm from your anglers.

'I hate Christmas,' they will cry plaintively. 'It's so boring.'

They
Simply
Fade Away

There comes a time in every angling circle when a sadness invades all the good-humoured camaraderie, for the death of one of the members will overshadow the frivolities on the charter-boat for several trips – despite the skipper allowing aboard ship a bottle or three of the deceased's favourite tipple so that his fellows can drink to the dear departed on the hour, every hour.

Jack Ray was well-known on our part of the Essex coast and rarely missed a fishing party in twenty years. He ventured out in all weathers and conditions even in his latter years, despite being chronologically challenged, looking like the old man of the sea and generally getting in the way until his talent for cookery was discovered and he was dispatched to the galley.

This suited him down to the ground for, as he grew older and found that he couldn't cope with the physical exertion necessary for serious angling, he continued to go out on the boats, purely for the company and to keep an eye on things while offering vast quantities of learned comments and advice.

There was one fine summer day aboard the *Skerry*

Belle when Alan Foster was the skipper and the calm, sunny conditions seemed to make up for the lack of excitement in the fishing. Jack was decrying the destruction of the environment, while sitting amidst the aromatic smog issuing from his pipe, and observing the creamy scud drifting slowly by on the tide. 'Floating orgasms' he declared it to be and it was a minute or two before the awestruck anglers realized that he had meant to say 'organisms'.

Becoming ship's cook constituted a valid excuse for his presence, besides giving him something useful to do, and he was considered to be an essential part of the crew, contributing to an important part of the anglers' day. Blinding curries, gourmet meals, duck, pheasant etc, were a speciality, as well as the more customary monster fry-ups in which he would include black pudding, sweetbreads, wild mushrooms and so on to liven them up a bit. He was able to produce much from limited ingredients coupled with a little imagination. A reasonable sweet and sour sauce emerged one day made from mustard, tomato ketchup and marmalade and the anglers swore that he made soup from his beard. Jack prided himself on his culinary ability and shared several cooking tips with the FWs in the pub afterwards – for the price of a small rum.

Back in the eighties he set himself up as patriarch of our angling crowd and organized the Jolly Fisherman Amateur Angling Society, applying for and receiving, on behalf of 'his boys', Specimen Award Certificates and the occasional medal from the NFSA. I was one of his 'boys' too, but it was only an honorary title – I have never deliberately caught a fish in my life. A sole somehow attached itself to my line once, many years ago, but it was a good half-hour before I realized it was there, so it doesn't really count.

Jack used to go along with the younger members on their conger-hunting trips, although he didn't actually fish for conger, preferring to dangle for other species, and became the proud captor of a 36lb 8oz cod, off Brixham, on 16 September 1987. It was the highlight of his fishing career and he was still describing the action, to anyone with the patience to listen – again – until his death a couple of months ago.

When 'his boys' began to produce boys – and girls – of their own, he looked after the youngsters on summer-boat trips, when their fathers were too busy catching skate or bass to offer more than a casual inquiry after the welfare of their offspring aboard boat. He would instruct the youngsters in baiting up or casting, reward the landing of an 8oz flounder with a chocolate bar and heap praise and encouragement upon young heads when they caught their first 'real' fish. He mopped up kids when they were sick, tucked them in when cold, fed them when hungry and handed them over, at the end of the day, safe and sound to mums waiting nervously at the wharf for the return of their juniors.

Awkward to the end, Jack died in February. We scattered his ashes to the four winds in a fresh north-easterly, from the deck of the *Skerry Belle*, to the sound of a lone saxophonist – Jack was a jazz musician when he wasn't fishing. It was one of the most moving scenes I have witnessed.

A number of wreaths had been retrieved from the Crematorium service, nurtured for a week and subsequently placed on the newly scrubbed deck of the boat. We had planned to throw them over the side at the appropriate time so, after a few words urging our departed friend to rest in peace, all the wreaths were dispatched except for ours which, because of its size (we had clubbed together and bought a three foot long wreath with JACK spelt out in bright yellow chrysanthemums) was the last one to go.

All the other floral tributes had drifted slowly towards the prow, flung a left and made their way out to sea. Not so, JACK. Colin Bond, our trusty skipper, used a boat hook in an effort to persuade our wreath, which clung to the side like a limpet, to move away. 'That old bugger,' groaned Colin. 'He doesn't want to go, does he?'

Eventually he managed to push JACK away and into the tide but, instead of following in the wake of its brethren, it carried straight on, in a direct line, towards the Southend Pier Head and the pub – The Jolly Fisherman – whereupon it hesitated for a good few minutes before doubling back and finally out to sea.

We took this personally. It was a sign, we concluded, to open and consume the crate of mulled wine which Jack's daughters had discovered gently mulling in his flat, lovingly prepared by him, for 'his boys', in anticipation of the next frost-bitten cod trip. The more probable, scientific and logical explanation for the course taken by our flowers – a freak current or a sudden change of wind direction – was dismissed as highly unlikely as we toasted our friend, each of us with our own silent memory of him, all the way back to the wharf.

Every fishing circle should include someone like Jack – if yours doesn't, then you are deprived, for the older members of a fishing crowd have much to offer. Make the most of the company of your elderly anglers; you won't realize how much you will miss them until they've gone. Maybe they do ramble on about their war escapades, how they caught giant shark off the Cornish coast in the old days but one of our circle summed it up, on hearing the news. He was tearful, he said, because never again would he be able to say 'For God's sake, Jack. Give your mouth a rest!'

Jack Ray was a wise and kind-hearted man and he will be sadly missed.

Old anglers never die, they simply wade away!
God bless. Dear boy.

Fish Meal

My angler and I have only ever had two serious rows in twenty-five years of marriage and they were both about fish. Not fishing, you understand. Just fish.

Hubby is a serious sea angler, apart from also being a serious coarse angler and possibly an equally serious game fisherman, given the chance, but the thing he is most serious about is the avoidance of eating his catch. Until comparatively recently he refused, point blank, to have anything to do with it after the gutting and filleting process. Wouldn't even taste it.

One Monday afternoon, early in our marriage, I decided to surprise him with a special meal, spending a couple of hours preparing poached cod with fresh prawns and a home-made bearnaise sauce – not that muck out of a jar, the real stuff. Ever made a bearnaise? It's like a glorified hollandaise and a bugger to get right. First of all you have to mix white wine, herb vinegar, chopped onion and parsley – reduce this lot by half, ie, boil it lots until it evaporates, and then add it to a combination of melted butter, egg yolks, sugar, salt and pepper – trying desperately not to allow it to curdle. This sauce, which took me a good hour to prepare was served over the cod and accompanied by creamed potatoes. Not mashed – creamed – through a hair sieve, hot milk, dollop of unsalted butter, freshly milled sea salt and black pepper and arranged artistically next to a green salad. I laid the table, lit candles, played soft music, made myself a cup of coffee and sat down to await my angler.

He walked into the dining room and switched on the main light saying 'It's a bit dark in here!' as I hurried kitchenwards to present my loved one with a designer meal.

'What's this?' he asked as I placed it gently in front of him.

'Whassit look like?' I replied, pre-menstrual tension rearing its ugly head. 'It's cod and it took ages to prepare. I had to . . .' but before I could bore him to tears with the recipe, he flipped.

'I'm not eating *that!*' he cried, aghast. 'That's fish! I've been working all day. I want meat when I come home – not this crap!' Was he in a paddy, or what?

Like I said, pre-menstrual, so I told him that if he didn't like it he could bugger off. And he did. I knew that he'd be back because he had left his cigarettes behind but he was gone a good couple of hours.

By the time he came home, we had both calmed down. He had realized just how much work I had put into this dinner and it had dawned on me that I had been extremely stupid. I knew that he didn't like fish, so why did I offer it? We kissed and made up, settled for egg and chips and I made my father eat the cod bearnaise the following day. The sauce was a bit lumpy by the time he got to it but he just scraped it to one side and tucked in. Dad would eat fish to the exclusion of everything else.

Some years later, whern our boys were eight and three years old, I made a similar mistake. We had been out for the day and we were all hot, tired and hungry so I irritably dumped the family at home, told hubby to butter some bread and get the plates ready while I drove to the chippy. Guess what I brought home? Cod and chips – stupid woman!

Hubby stormed out in a huff after frayed tempers had finally torn and the kids, seated either side of the table, looked at each other in disbelief.

'Oh, Si,' David said sadly to this little brother. 'We might never see Dad again!' Simon looked confused, fidgeted on his seat and, not really understanding the seriousness of his brother's remark, allowed hunger to get the better of him.

'Can I have his chips, Mum?' he asked innocently.

'And me,' piped up Dave, who was never backward in coming forward if spare food was about.

Nowadays, things have changed. My Chief Angler will eat fish, now and again, but I had to introduce him to it gradually, beginning with a small portion as a starter – before his steak and chips – then, as we went through a patch being short of money, as a main course. I don't push my luck though. A fish meal once every few weeks is all he can tolerate.

Recipes

Do not, under any circumstances, try offering your anglers a few cheese sandwiches and a flask of tea to take out on the boat for a day's fishing. They will snigger derisively and, in the small hours, attempt to smuggle out the pre-cooked Sunday joint or the fruits of your last baking day which you naively assumed were safely hidden at the back of the freezer.

There are various recipes that you can prepare to prevent this subterfuge. It is well worth the effort, for a few snacks that *you* have made will prevent your anglers from raiding the fridge/store-cupboard and they will always purloin far more food than you are prepared to part with – just for a day's fishing. Have you seen what they can get through in a matter of twelve hours or so? You could feed a family for a week on what they pinch from the larder.

A word of warning if you get enthusiastic about sausage rolls – on no account leave them to cool when there is anyone in the house. I once repeated my recipe three times before I could rescue from starving mouths sufficient sausage rolls to see me over Christmas.

In the winter they will enjoy a pot of chilli to take out on the boat. It fits into a wide-necked Thermos and it looks as if someone has thrown up in the flask when you pour it out but the anglers don't seem to mind – particularly if you send along some small mutton pies to go with it. They find it too much trouble to cut a portion of a large pie and when you imagine what they have had their hands in and on, to hold a lump of pie for too long has to be some kind of health risk.

The few suggested recipes which follow are easy and cheapish. Try them – your anglers will think you are wonderful!

Steak en Croute

Fry onions, mushrooms and one-inch strips of the cheapest, flash-fry steak for about five minutes or until the onions are soft.

Roll out a square of short pastry, throw the filling on it, fold it over, stamp on the edges so the juices can't escape and bake for about 20 minutes, medium oven, until golden brown.

Allow to cool, cut into fingers and wrap in tinfoil. If you make half a dozen at a time they can be frozen for future fishing trips. Just don't let on where, in the freezer, they can be located or you'll have to do it all again. They will be eaten in between trips, meals or slices of bread.

Quiches

Since you have made pastry anyway you can line a few quiche tins and hurl leftover bits from the fridge into them, eg, a couple of cold, lonely sausages (sliced), a few rashers of bacon, the last slice of salami, bits of second-hand corned beef, just past their best mushrooms etc.

Cover the evidence with a mixture of beaten eggs, a little milk, a handful each of grated cheddar and parmesan and few chopped herbs.

Cook in a moderate oven until almost set. Slice tomatoes and arrange artistically round the edges – bake for a further five minutes or so. Freeze or not.

Sausage Bites

Mix together a couple of pounds of sausage meat with a cooked, chopped onion and some chopped, fresh sage, chives or thyme – all three if you are feeling frolicsome.

Roll out strips of pastry about four inches wide by as long as it stretches. Heap the filling down the middle, roll the whole thing over into one long sausage – brush the top with beaten egg and cut it into one-inch chunks.

Bake for about 15 minutes. Makes about 60.

Thick Soup (as opposed to intelligent soup)

I usually save the stock made from boiled-up chicken carcasses or beef bones but if you can't be bothered to do that you can use stock cubes.

Boil a pound of potatoes and an onion in a couple of pints of stock until the spuds are cooked. Sling it through a liquidizer.

Pour into a large non-stick pot. Add a few sliced carrots, a handful of barley or lentils, a few frozen peas, beans or whatever you've got, cabbage leaves, a chopped leek, any vegetables will do – and simmer for about half an hour – lid off or it won't thicken up.

Chilli

Chopped onion and squashed garlic into a pot. Add a

couple of pounds of minced beef, two tins of tomatoes, one medium-sized tin of tomato purée, two teaspoons-ful of chilli power and a *small* pinch of cayenne pepper – or cheat and buy two packets of instant chilli mix instead.

Simmer for half an hour then add a large tin each of red kidney beans and butter beans. Continue to simmer for another 20 minutes.

Individual Mutton Pies

These small pies are much more convenient for your angler than one large one and do you want them to catch cod or don't you?

Pastry cases as in mince-pies but fill them with a mixture of chopped leftovers eg, cold lamb, diced car-rot, onion and potato which you have moistened with surplus-to-requirements gravy.

Put lids on, brush with beaten egg and bake for 15 to 20 minutes until golden.

Then there are the times when you will be expected to cook the catch. Try these painless ways:

Skate, Thornbacks etc

You may be forced to dream up a recipe because all you have in the store cupboard at the end of a salary month that happens to fall on a skating weekend is garlic, herbs and butter and, particularly if the captors are under sixteen, they want to eat the fruits of their fishing trip *now*! I speak from experience.

Skate in Garlic Butter

Splash a tablespoonful of olive oil into a biggish pan

and melt an ounce or two of butter into it – the oil prevents the butter from burning. Add a clove or two of garlic, cruelly squashed. Incidentally, while on the subject of garlic, a clove is a crescent-shaped segment – *not* the whole thing. I gave this recipe to a thick friend who rang me the next day complaining that it was 'too foreign' so her family couldn't eat it. She had put in a whole head of the stuff – silly person!

Salt and a liberal helping of freshly ground, black pepper is added at this point. Swish all this around in the pan for a few seconds, then shove the skate in.

Cook over moderate flame – moderate glow if you have electric – for about five minutes each side or until you can scrape the flesh from the bones without spraining a wrist.

Throw a handful of chopped parsley or tarragon over the top – to give the illusion that you have put some effort into it – and serve with new potatoes dosed with a little mayonnaise and accompanied by peas or anything else green that you may have lurking in the freezer.

Herring

These are never brought home fresh from the sea. They are bought from the local fishmonger at considerable expense and kept in suspended animation until they can be thrown over the side of a boat in a usually vain attempt to snare skate.

You may be able to steal a few from the bait section of the family freezer but, if you stoop to this level, you must pretend that you have queued all morning in the pouring rain in order to acquire them. Your crime can go unnoticed for weeks if you don't mention your prowess as a herring cook too often.

Served with wholemeal toast and garnished with fried onions, they are the cheapest fish supper known to woman, but only if you aren't found out.

Split them from neck to tail, lay them skin side down and squash them severely until they are flat. Season with plenty of lemon juice, salt and pepper and shove them under a hot grill for about five minutes each side. Don't forget to season the other side when you turn them over.

Herring Roes

Soft roes should be eaten for breakfast after being stir-fried for about five minutes. Served on wholemeal toast, accompanied by rashers of crisp, smoked bacon and fried tomatoes they can make a wonderful start to anybody's day. They never do in our house, my anglers prefer cornflakes for breakfast, but they should do.

Bass

Wear your best clothes and a pinny for this one, and make the most of it because you won't have the opportunity very often.

First, place two bottles of Chablis in the fridge. Lay the dining-room table with a Victorian, white linen tablecloth and the best china. Dim the lights and make for the kitchen.

Take a large sheet of aluminium foil, place the bass reverently upon it, stuff its vacated stomach with a mixture of mushrooms, prawns and garlic, and loads of black pepper. Pin the edges of the opening together with cocktail sticks, wrap the whole caboodle up in foil making sure it can't escape and force it into a medium hot oven. About an hour and a half for a seven-pound fish should to it. Or three-quarters of an hour for a four pounder – which you are more likely to get.

Open the Chablis and serve the bass with crusty French bread and a green salad.

Dab and Sole

Fillets of sole or dab are a cinch to cook. Fried in breadcrumbs with lemon wedges, or stuffed, rolled up, and baked they make a delightful supper dish on summer evenings. They can be stuffed with practically anything providing it is mixed with butter and a few seasoned soft breadcrumbs to give them a bit of bulk. I have found that half a dozen dabs, filleted and naked, will not satisfy three ravenous anglers, not without a spot of padding – you can always throw in the odd prawn, mushroom or tomato to make it a bit more exciting.

Lay the fillets flat and put just enough stuffing in each so that it doesn't fall out of the ends when you roll them up. Secure with cocktail sticks – wooden ones, please, the plastic ones melt and you have to fish them out with a spoon – it ruins the symmetry of the completed dish.

Rolled-up fillets then go into a shallow dish with a quarter of a pint of skimmed milk poured over the top – or single cream if you can stand the cholesterol – scrunch black peppercorns over the lot, cover and bake in a medium oven for about 20 minutes. Serve with creamed potatoes. Garnish with chopped parsley, you will need some colour, without it this dish looks like everyone's back garden after a blizzard.

Cod

The variations for cooking cod are unlimited. All that is required is a little imagination.

Cod in Anything Sauce

If you cook cod, or any fish come to that, in a microwave it retains more moisture but you can cook it in a conventional oven if you make sure it is covered up. When the fish is cooked allow it to cool and remove any skin or bones from the meat.

Now you can knock up a basic white sauce and flavour it with cheese or parsley or garlic, onion, mustard, anchovy, eggs (hard-boiled and chopped), practically anything that you have handy. Mix the flaked cod into the sauce and throw it onto a shallow bed of cooked cauliflower that you prepared earlier – preferably in a pie-dish.

Pipe, or scoop if you have lost the piping-bag again, mashed potatoes around the edge and either freeze it or bake it in a hottish oven until the potatoes are brown and crunchy on top.

Instead of making your own sauce, you can cheat and use a packet soup mix but only use half the amount of water recommended to make up the soup, otherwise the mashed potato will subside into the liquid and you'll have to call it a chowder.

Whole fillets of cod can be served with a cheese sauce, sauté potatoes and a green vegetable but plain cheese sauce is a bit boring so I do mine like this:

Fry three or four rashers of smoked bacon until crisp. Chop them up and put them to one side. Knock up the usual white sauce with butter, flour and milk. Add a teaspoonful of made English mustard, black pepper, the chopped bacon, grated cheddar and a handful of parmesan. Also good for making macaroni taste halfway decent.

Then there is always the old standby:

Cod in Batter

Mix together two or three ounces of self-raising flour and two eggs seasoned with salt and pepper. Add another egg if the batter is too thick. *No milk.* Drag the cod fillets through this mess and fry in medium hot oil for five minutes each side. Serve with chips, peas and tartare sauce that you have bought at a supermarket.

Cod Steaks

Occasionally you may be presented with a cod which is fat enough to be cut into steaks. You can bake them in chicken stock, white wine and garlic. They will take a good three-quarters of an hour in a medium oven so I usually throw a pan of potatoes in at the same time to roast – then all you have to do is open a tin of peas or something. Easy.

Whiting

There are only two things to do with whiting. Feed them to the cat or make –

Whiting Fish Cakes

Cook the fillets (or whole fish) in a little milk. Remove the bones and put the flesh into a large bowl. Add a level tablespoonful, per pound of fish, of matzos meal, a quarter-pint of the cooking liquid and a handful of finely chopped parsley.

Add two eggs to this mess and season with salt and pepper. Leave it in the fridge to partially solidify for at least half an hour while you make the sauce. If you don't chill it, you will have more mixture up your arms than in the fish cakes.

Meanwhile, make a tomato and garlic sauce. This is a

vital ingredient – to give the whiting some identity.

Tomato and Garlic Sauce tastes wonderful, everyone thinks you are brilliant and it's as easy as opening a tin.

Chop a small onion finely and sling it into a frying pan containing a tablespoonful of olive oil. Add a couple of squashed garlic cloves, two teaspoonsful of dried basil or a handful of fresh, open a tin of tomatoes, chop them up and throw them into the pan. Simmer for about 20 minutes, by which time your previously refrigerated, glutinous mixture should be cold enough to handle.

Vegetable oil into another frying pan, grab handfuls (or should it be handsful) of the now less-sloppy-fish-cake mess and drop them into a bowl of flour. Shake off the excess and fry for about three minutes each side.

Pour the sauce into a gravy boat and serve separately. There's always one member of the family who will demand the ketchup because your tomato sauce 'has got lumps in it'.

PART FIVE

Serendipity

A Glimmer
of Insight

There was a time, in the dark and distant and even extending up to the recent past, when it all seemed such a waste of valuable time. Pointless to be sitting beside a lake or on a river bank when there were so many pressing jobs to be done at home. Washing, ironing, baking, cleaning would beckon and I would fidget guiltily or just sit, resigned to a full day of inactivity, smile when spoken to and pretend patience until it was time to go home.

For over twenty years the pattern had been the same, relieved only by our three months close season; I would read, struggle with crossword puzzles or write down amusing incidents to relieve the monotony of the day while my husband instructed our two, then embryo, anglers in the art of carp fishing. No one ever suggested that I should take part for, they said, I was only a girly and therefore incapable of taking it all in. They were probably right and so I did what I was best at – dispensing food, binding wounds or muttering comforting phrases when things went wrong.

The embryos eventually grew into fully competent

anglers and still I watched, without seeing, just record-ing the obviously funny bits for my own amusement and for magazine editors with a sense of humour. Until several months ago, when I spoke to a Wise Man of the North, a certain Tim Paisley, editor and carp angler of some renown, who offered me startling but, as it turned out, very sound advice.

'Don't try to write humour all the time,' he told me. 'Go and sit with them, by the water and let your pen wander – look around you and write what you feel.'

I took this advice to heart, remaining unconvinced that anything remarkable would come of it, but those few words have opened up a whole new world. Only now, for the first time in nearly a quarter of a century, am I beginning to understand the compulsion of my menfolk to be beside a stretch of water with Mother Nature all around and elusive fish in front of them – and all because of a short conversation with a man whom I had never met.

Capturing these beautiful creatures is an art. It is not, as it always appeared to me, just a matter of slinging in bait on a hook and waiting. There's a challenge here, a kind of primeval hunting instinct takes over. A certain rapport has to be achieved with the fish, his habits must be studied, his whims catered for; he must be stalked and outwitted before he is caught and after-wards treated with respect and gentleness before being returned to his habitat, sound in wind and limb, having undergone the minimum of stress while smiling for the inevitable photograph.

Watching my sons, through this newly acquired and clearer vision, has been a revelation. They are normally boistrous, noisy and careless but at the water's edge they are quiet, compassionate towards their prey and have an unspoken but close communication between themselves, which would be less amazing to me had I not witnessed fights 'to the death' because one of them was certain that the other had been given four more cornflakes or half an inch more sausage. Bait secrets are shared, tackle in a communal box – not once did I hear 'That's *mine!*' – aid offered in removing excess rods from the water during play and netting undertaken, almost as an honour, when the fish is brought in close enough to the shingle.

There is an undercurrent of friendly rivalry among most anglers which extends beyond the family groups but also a common bond. You have only to see the grudging admiration offered by fellow anglers to the captor of a thirty-pound carp to appreciate this kind of comradeship. Complete strangers will sit on the fringe of your encampment, after an excitement of landing a big one, carrying on low-voiced conversations about baits or other venues fished – and then wish you luck as they return to their own swim.

In the competitive rat race that most of us are compelled to live in today, it's a welcome change. Inevitably there are always a few who turn green with envy and bitterness if someone catches a bigger fish than they – let's face it, there's always at least one – but I can only speak from experience and so far, so good.

After a couple of hours of keen observation while they baited up the swims and held *sotto voce* discussions on where, how and when the carp would possibly bite, the sheer tranquillity of my surroundings overtook me. I began to relax and enjoy the helicopter flights of vivid dragonflies, the ungainly attempts of moorhens to walk upon too fragile lily-beds and the Zeppelin-like drone of huge bumble bees with pointy faces who almost waved a greeting as they rumbled tipsily past.

On previous occasions I would produce a picnic

around lunchtime. Freshly ironed tablecloth, food laid out prettily and a demand that my anglers at least perform lip service to my efforts even if their attention was still at the edge of the reeds. This time, there were no interruptions on this warm summer afternoon and eventually they wandered over, one at a time and at varying intervals, to my corner to see if I was OK, no doubt wondering why I remained so unruffled and calm. The youngest asked me if I had a headache, then reassured that I was perfectly well, grabbed a cheese roll and headed back waterwards to regale his father and brother with the unbelievable story that his mother seemed to be having a good time.

Yes, they did catch carp but I wasn't listening to their muted cries of 'twenty-two' or 'sixteen and a half' as they weighed and scrutinized their fish. The patterns on the backs of mirrors are beautiful and all of them are different – I had never noticed it before. We are all aware that no two creatures on God's earth are the same, the Doppelgänger theory is only a myth – but every single carp in the universe being unique, and all other living things for that matter, makes you feel quite humble if you think about it.

Strangely, I was reluctant to go home. My anglers, knowing of my restlessness towards the end of the day, usually make placatory statements at this time. 'Ten minutes and we'll pack up' – they mean half an hour – or 'Why don't you go back to the car, we'll pack up and meet you there in half an hour' – they mean an hour and a half. They exchanged quizzical glances when I calmly told them there was no rush.

One day, I'll ask them if I can borrow a rod for a while – then I can discover for myself what it's really all about.

Glossary – A Few Angling Terms (and What They Really Mean)

Angling Club
Used to berate your anglers when all else fails *or* a group of anglers.

Arsley Bombs
Used to relieve haemorrhoids caused by sitting on stone piers *or* a type of weight.

Artificial Flies
The razor-bladed slits cut down the front of your best tights in winter *or* imitation insects.

Bait Box
Tupperware.

Bar Spinner
Tall storyteller in the pub *or* a type of lure.

Barbel
Lady angler in the pub *or* a species of fish.

Bird's Nest
No. 7 on Chinese takeaway menus. Used after a family day out at the river *or* a hopelessly tangled line.

Bite-alarm
A condition experienced by engrossed, young anglers when they realize they have not eaten crisps or chocolate for more

than twenty minutes *or* an electronic beeper.

Bite Indicator

Gesture made by anglers on river banks, ie pointing finger at mouth when hungry *or* a visual warning device.

Bivvy

Anglers can't pronounce bivouac.

Blank

Expressions on anglers' faces at any given time except when a fish is caught *or* a length of carbon fibre used to build a rod *or* a fishless day.

Boilie

What FWs do when trapped at a venue and the weather turns unseasonably warm *or* spherical baits for carp.

Butt Pad

Scrap paper on which to write shopping lists, eg *but* I need that farmhouse loaf tonight *or* a harness worn to hold lower section of rod.

Carp

What they do when they lose a fish *or* Common, Mirror, Crucian, Leather etc.

Carp Ears

These develop when you have heard yet another account of the capture *or* bite-alarm attachments.

Casters (Oiled)

What an efficiently run angling household must run *or* on maggots, at chrysalis stage.

Cloudbaiting

Casts thrown so high you'd think the fish lived in the trees *or* sloppy ground-bait.

Coarse Fishing

Shouting abuse at other water users *or* fresh-water fishing.

Colman

Who they resemble after bait-

	digging in black, sticky mud *or* the trade name for anglers' portable stoves.
Conger	A dance executed all along the South Devon coast.
Disgorger	Opposite to Datgorger *or* a hook remover.
Drip-feeding	What your angler may need after you have used the Angling Club *or* bait presentation.
Dry Fly Fishing	Only going in the water up to the knees *or* with a fly on top of the water.
Fishing Licence	Similar to poetic licence but only applies to the size of the fish.
Ground-bait	Maggots spilt on the river bank *or* assorted cereals mixed with water.
Hollow Glass	Seemingly what their beer is poured into *or* a type of rod.
Jig	Final movement of the 'I've really caught one this time' ritual *or* the lure method.
Lobworms	Worms to be thrown in the river *or* a type of worm.
Lugworm	Worms carried around near salt water *or* another type of worm.
Match Rod	My rod's bigger than your rod *or* a lightweight rod.
Mealworms	Worms that somehow get involved with your sandwiches *or* yet another type of worm.
Mixed	What most fishing widows' feelings are towards their

anglers *or* assorted maggots in the same pot.

Monkey Climber — Your youngest, bored-stiff child *or* a bite indicator.

Mussels — You must develop these to help them to carry all that gear.

Paternoster — The Lord's Prayer, frequently muttered by FWs, particularly near liquid, *or* a type of rig.

Pinky — Affectionate name for light red maggots.

Pollack — What anglers call other anglers *or* a species of fish.

Priest — What Catholic anglers look as if they need after a long session *or* a lead baton used to kill edible fish.

Ragworm — University students, of no moral worth, during one week of the year *or* worms with legs.

Rig — Suggested result of some competitions *or* to set up hook, weight and bait.

Rod Pod — Race track *or* a multiple rod holder.

Rod Rest — Time for a beer *or* a cleft stick.

Roker — Term of endearment for skate.

Rubbers (packets of) — Yes, probably those *or* minute rubber bands.

Rubby Dubby — Where they end up legless after all piscatorial encounters *or* unspeakable ground-bait.

Shakespeare Box — Part of a theatre – where you will never persuade your angler to set foot *or* the trade-name for a tackle box.

Shellfish — Most of 'em are.

Snap Tackle	The noise made by anglers' breakfasts *or* wire trace.
Spoon	No chance, they're too busy fishing *or* to lure.
Squid	What your angler gives you when you want a drink in the pub. You'll have to get it yourself.
Swim	You must never do this anywhere near your angler *or* a section of water so called 'cos fish . . . er . . . swim in it.
Swivel	What all heads do when another angler catches a fish *or* a little metal thingy.
Tackle Box	Your inherited Edwardian picnic hamper.
Tope	Colour assumed by some anglers aboard ship, usually the morning after *or* the shark family.
Trace	What we occasionally wish they'd disappear without *or* a part of a rig.
Twitcher Wheel	Angling executive's anti-stress toy *or* an attachment for a bite alarm.
Uptide Fishing	Fishing in the better stretches of the river *or* a method of sea casting in shallow water.
Waggler	Inexperienced and nervous angler *or* a type of float.
Wet Fly Fishing	Waist deep in the river *or* with a fly under the water.
Wreck Fishing	Label that should be attached to an angler who has an early start after a party the night before *or* fishing over sunken ships.

Anglers' Ailments

Anglers are never ill. They may develop acute and desperate influenza mid-week and demand constant nursing – you know the kind of thing – tea, toast and lightly boiled eggs with soldiers, progressing to a large Vindaloo with all the trimmings by teatime. All meals to be served on trays to the bedside – but they are *never* ill enough to cancel a fishing trip.

By the weekend, usually Friday evening, they are sufficiently recovered to totter down to the pub to make arrangements for a day or two out on the boat, or camped beside a lake, by way of convalescence – they have to go to the pub, by the way, these things can't be discussed over the phone and most of the anglers I know find it next to impossible to hold a coherent conversation without something held in their right hand – usually a pint, but not always.

A less relaxing sport can be hard to find. The general consensus is that anglers sit around all day gazing at the horizon and dreaming of the philosophy of life. In reality they are constantly on the move, fetching and carrying, retackling, rebaiting, recasting, trying to find a better mark/swim and so on.

The act of playing and landing a couple of big ones can be as physically exhausting as a squash game. The ensuing injuries sometimes include backache, frontache, strained muscles, ligaments or other parts, the occasional hernia, and not forgetting increased blood pressure – this especially if the almost captured prize escapes – but nothing short of death will stop them from fishing. I know of an angler who had his right arm in plaster from fingertip to elbow but who still managed, with a little help from his friends, to go out on the boat on the fishing weekends and catch cod.

Severe back pain can prevent the garden from being dug over for weeks on end – but a short walk out on the mud brings about a miracle cure and the lug/rag-worms are harvested with ease. Unfortunately the cure doesn't last very long for as soon as they set foot back into the garden the 'back's gone again' and they're in agony. Until tomorrow when the sea air, topped up with 'one of Jack's specials' – which consists of everything that isn't nailed to the deck being thrust into a large pan and fried at a hundred miles an hour – will quickly put everything to rights.

And have you noticed that their digestive problems are never caused by a surfeit of lager or an excess of fried 'cabin' food, but it must be that the lovingly prepared casserole and steamed vegetables that you served up for dinner was too rich – it's the only explanation. Well, the only one that they'll admit to anyway.

Here are a few medical terms that may prove useful. Every angler suffers from all of these at various times:

Allergies   Digging the garden, decorating, taking out the rubbish, etc.

Amnesia	Often experienced by anglers around birthdays and anniversaries.
Arthritis	Caused by listening to an account of Arthur's 'one that got away' for the n'th time.
Blackwater Fever	Compulsion to fish around the Bradwell-on-Sea, Essex area.
Carpal Tunnel Syndrome	Nervous exhaustion brought on by the constant disappearance of crucians into the reeds.
Deafness	What all anglers suffer from when spoken to about anything other than fishing.
Dehydration	Very serious problem meaning lack of water.
Delusions	False judgements believed to be true by the anglers, especially when arguing with stewards at weigh-ins.
Dipsomania	A compulsion to dip various items in water, eg, maggots, sweetcorn, luncheon meat etc.
Drink Problems	Can't get enough. The pubs aren't open. Forgot the bottle opener. There's a wasp in the can of lager etc.
Dropsy	Clumsiness, usually suffered after several pints of something, also may occur when fishing in sub-zero temperatures.
Fissure	Angler.
Genes	Standard item of clothing for anglers.
Greenstick Fracture	The new rod is broken already.
Hangover	What FWs do to the railings on wharves, landing piers etc.

Hydrophobia	Fear of being unable to find enough water to fish in.
Premature Ejaculation	Passionately exclaiming 'I've got one – it feels like a biggun' – just as the monster drops off/bites through the hook and falls back into the sea/lake.
Prostate	How they feel at the end of a fishing trip.
Rash	As in don't do anything ... (like sign a marriage certificate).
Salmonella	Irresistible urge to throw things at big fish in Scotland.
Sternum	The back of the boat.
Wind	No, not flatulence, although having mentioned it ... but the strong gale force one that begins suddenly an hour before cast off. This causes untold misery and great suffering – especially to FWs.
Worms	Involuntary reflex which makes them try to collect as many as possible before the tide comes in.
Yaws	As in 'What's?' They all suffer from this.

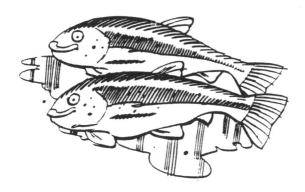